**Letters Home**

Box 30 M

August, 2021

For you, Marlene V. Gade,
with gratitude for our
friendship and with
best wishes always.

X Kelly

Sheldon Lewis

# Letters Home: A Jewish Chaplain's Vietnam Memoir

Hakodesh Press

Publisher:
Hakodesh Press
is a trademark of
Dodo Books Indian Ocean Ltd., member of the OmniScriptum S.R.L Publishing group
str. A.Russo 15, of. 61, Chisinau-2068, Republic of Moldova Europe
Printed at: see last page
**ISBN: 978-3-639-79484-7**

# Letters Home: A Jewish Chaplain's Vietnam Memoir

"When I first met Rabbi Shelly Lewis in the jungles in Vietnam, I felt he was truly a man of God. Months later, that feeling was reinforced as he stood by my hospital bed in an evacuation hospital where I struggled to survive. After being critically wounded, I specifically asked the Army to get Rabbi Shelly. He came and stayed with me until I was well enough to be transferred. I KNOW his comforting presence helped me to survive my devastating wounds. We became lifelong friends.

Rabbi Shelly Lewis has finally written this account of his year as an Army chaplain in Vietnam. This long overdue memoir tells how Rabbi Shelly, along with fellow Jewish and non-Jewish soldiers, kept faith, hope and feelings of home alive amidst the sorrows and chaos of war."

– LLOYD KANTOR, Wounded Vietnam Veteran


"A band of brothers, a booby trap ignited in Vietnam with devastating injuries, the selfless valor of comrades-in-arms, the skill of Army medical teams, the intimate letters between the Jewish chaplain and his wife, despite the physical catastrophe, Lloyd's profound will to live sustained by the tenacious love of his devoted wife.

Fifty years later five brothers, separated by the pandemic reunite on screen. Shelly Lewis's memoir is a testament to the soul and faith that endured over the years; the bond that transcended war and revealed the phenomenal, persevering, healing bond, the power of presence. This heartful, wise tribute, is must reading."

– REV. DOUGLAS HUNEKE, author of *Moses of Rovno*


"In my experience, most clergy are accustomed to teaching, preaching, lecturing, informing and sermonizing. After all, "Rabbi" means teacher. As we traveled around Nam I found that most soldiers just wanted to talk to someone who would listen and empathize with them. We were serving our Country in a very confusing war, place, time and circumstance which most of us did not understand and/or support. It was important to speak with an open, objective, person who you could confide in and not be judged. The successful, most respected Chaplains, those who the men could relate to, were of this ilk. Certainly, Chaplain Lewis learned this quickly and his active listening skills and nurturing personality made him one of the most respected of the clergy in IICorps."

– ED FINKELSTEIN, Chaplain's Assistant to Rabbi Lewis in Vietnam

"I have had the privilege of reading the Vietnam Memoir by Rabbi Sheldon Lewis recalling his time as a U.S. Army Chaplain during the Vietnam conflict. In this heartwarming memoir, Rabbi Lewis is able to reconstruct a vivid picture of life in the military as both a chaplain and a servicemember. Far-flung Jews anxiously awaiting the arrival of the chaplain was a common experience. Conducting services, rites, and ceremonies under the most trying conditions marks the agility of chaplains to adapt to the congregation wherever they may be. Bringing his story to light brings to the fore the work of military chaplains who work tirelessly to meet the needs of servicemembers scattered around the world. Hopefully, this book will serve as a constant reminder of the vital role played by military chaplains of every stripe and color."

– RABBI MAURICE KAPROW, Commander, US Navy (Retired)

*For Lloyd and Loretta Kantor,
extraordinary models of courage,
resilience, and devotion.*

# Contents

INTRODUCTION   7

CHAPTER 1: The Context – The Late Sixties   11

CHAPTER 2: Entering Service   14

CHAPTER 3: Fort Lewis   16

CHAPTER 4: Arrival in Vietnam   24

CHAPTER 5: My Assignment   26

CHAPTER 6: Building Sanctuaries in Time   31

CHAPTER 7: One on One   64

CHAPTER 8: Sex, Drugs, and Race   78

CHAPTER 9: Interfaith Relationships   82

CHAPTER 10: Connections to the Vietnamese   86

CHAPTER 11: Care from the Jewish Community   93

CHAPTER 12: Coping   96

CHAPTER 13: Going Home   100

CHAPTER 14: The Aftermath   102

CHAPTER 15: Final Thoughts   107

ACKNOWLEDGEMENTS   111

*Zoom reunion of platoon – 50 years later*

# Introduction

*November 16, 1970*

While on patrol on a hill in the northern sector of South Vietnam, Lloyd Kantor's platoon, Charlie Company, 1/52nd Infantry, Americal Division, triggered two explosive booby traps. The results were catastrophic. Two soldiers were killed. Lloyd was severely hurt as were two others. Despite the risk of triggering other booby traps, Bill Frankovich heroically carried him down the hill in a poncho to a waiting helicopter which whisked him away to the evacuation hospital at Chu Lai in a frenzied attempt to save his life.

*November 16, 2020*

On the screen before me were Lloyd and Loretta Kantor, four of Lloyd's buddies (Richard Gibbs, Paul (Mac) McClellan, William (Bill) Frankovich, and Furman Conard) and myself. Loretta had arranged this virtual reunion as a surprise for Lloyd. Only the rampant coronavirus had prevented a gathering in person.

At that tragic moment a half century earlier, the lives of all the men on the screen were bound together as brothers. I listened to their reminiscences of that traumatic day. Lloyd repeatedly thanked Bill for saving his life. Their memories were vivid – of the terrain, of the height of the elephant grass which made it exceedingly difficult to detect more booby traps, and of the urgency to save Lloyd. Being together made the memories of the distant past come alive.

. . . .

Returning from a visit to Phu Cat on Tuesday, November 17, 1970, my supervisor, Chaplain (Col) Joe Andrews immediately called me into his office. An urgent message had been delivered that a wounded soldier had asked for me. It was Lloyd Kantor. He had been evacuated to a hospital in

Chu Lai, far to the north and outside of my region. I was to leave immediately. A reservation had already been made on a flight. I did not know the extent of his injuries. I was on my way within minutes.

I clearly remembered Lloyd. We were first introduced in the bush near An Khe where his infantry unit was standing down to rest and resupply. He was the only Jew in his platoon, an engaging, upbeat young man with an unmistakable New York accent. He was cheerful, totally without complaints, and appreciative of the smallest things. I was immediately drawn to him. I recall conducting a brief service outdoors with Lloyd as the only other Jew present, but some of his buddies were curious and attended, too. I have a photo of a friendly monkey, adopted by a local unit, who readily climbed onto my neck and shoulders.

A short time later during the High Holidays, we gathered about 200 troops in Cam Ranh Bay for services and camaraderie. Lloyd was able to participate enthusiastically. His outgoing, friendly nature made him a magnet for others. In that crowd, he stood out. Our friendship grew.

The night flight north was turbulent. It was the monsoon season, and we traveled in a heavy storm. At some point, circling in preparation for landing, the cabin filled up with a heavy, odorless fog. It was otherworldly, reflecting the somber nature of my journey. It was scary, but everyone was completely silent and outwardly calm.

Before seeing him, I described the sense of helplessness that I felt in a letter to my wife:

*How bad it is I don't know just yet, but I fear it is bad . . . This is so tragic,*

*Lloyd Kantor before being wounded*

*and I feel so inadequate. But I will do my best to cheer him and be strong at least for him to see. Coming up here, I felt so disjointed, bewildered. Somehow I had felt or hoped that I would be spared these crises, but they are so real, and they do happen every day and take such a toll . . . It all seemed so distant . . . but now . . .*

Finally, and thankfully, I arrived at the hospital and went immediately to see Lloyd. Nothing in my life had prepared me for what I would behold. Lloyd lay before me having had all four limbs amputated. He had lost an eye as well among other injuries. He was fully conscious and aware. He was hovering between life and death.

These are the words I wrote to my wife the next day:

*I've seen almost too much. Lloyd really was hurt badly, but he is amazing everyone with his determination to live. You have no idea what an inspiration he is to everyone around. No one expected him to come through, but he seems to have an unlimited amount of determination to make a comeback and something out of his life . . . These days have been so trying. I so wished this would never happen. Were it not for his own amazing will, I don't know how I could have helped. All I've been doing is going in every few hours, talking, reading his mother's and his girlfriend's letters to him, praying a little with him. He seems so glad I came. I guess I'm the only familiar face.*

The impact of that reunion fifty years later awakened a flood of memories for me. It was then that I decided to write about my year as a chaplain in Vietnam. Lloyd's tragedy and his determination to live were perhaps the most dramatic and heart-wrenching of my year of service, but there are so many other encounters and experiences that now seemed worthy of sharing.

There is another reason why this memoir was so long delayed. At the reunion zoom meeting, everyone told of returning to an indifferent if not hostile homecoming. Close family and friends extended a welcome; but, for the most part, returning soldiers were ignored if not vilified. Very few were interested in hearing the account of a harrowing tour of duty.

My homecoming was similarly muted. Of course, I relished being reunited with my newlywed wife and family. Yet, in the atmosphere of war protest, I was greeted with silence. In fact, I served as a community rabbi for decades before I felt it was time to speak of my time in Vietnam as a chaplain. As vivid and traumatic as those days were for me, I repressed them because I sensed no one really wanted to listen.

Now it is different. The moral assessment of the war has not changed, but those who served especially during a period of the draft are treated belatedly with respect. Those veterans did not declare war; they were among the best and brightest of their generation who chose not to resist their government's call. Now retrospectively they are treated with dignity.

Personally, I have felt this sea change. I've been invited to speak. I no longer hesitate to wear a hat which identifies me as a Vietnam vet. When people respond with "Thank you for your service," I know they intend to convey gratitude. Now I feel empowered to write. As I sit down to begin my memoir, every new day is a fifty-year anniversary of one more day of my tour of duty in Vietnam.

With the passage of half a century, my memory has surely eroded. Were it not for the daily letters I wrote to my wife and the reel-to-reel audio tapes we exchanged, I would not be able to recapture my tenure in Vietnam accurately. I have not reread them nor replayed them until now. Letters and tapes are my journal.

# CHAPTER 1

# The Context – The Late Sixties

עוֹשֶׂה שָׁלוֹם בִּמְרוֹמָיו הוּא יַעֲשֶׂה שָׁלוֹם עָלֵינוּ
וְעַל כָּל יִשְׂרָאֵל
וְאִמְרוּ: אָמֵן.

Oseh shalom bimromav, Hu ya-a-seh shalom oleynu
v'al kol Yisrael v'imru omen.

May the One who creates peace on high bring peace
to us and to all Israel (and to all the inhabitants of
the world). And we say: Amen.

*– Chanted with his original melody
by Rabbi Abraham Joshua Heschel at an anti-war
protest in 1969*

I was an unlikely candidate for the military chaplaincy. I came of age as a student at the Jewish Theological Seminary in the upper West Side of Manhattan. The neighborhood teemed with war protest. My teacher and mentor was Rabbi Abraham Joshua Heschel who, along with Dr. Martin Luther King, formed Clergy and Laity Concerned for Vietnam, perhaps the most potent voice of key religious leaders against the war. In fact, it was Rabbi Heschel who prevailed on Dr. King to join the war protest despite the risk to the civil rights movement of breaking with the White House. I was present at Riverside Church on April 4, 1967, in New York when Dr. King first emerged as a war critic with his friend Rabbi Heschel beside him. I watched and listened intently as together they spoke eloquently against the war. I took part in war protest myself.

I was shielded from the draft as a divinity student. Clergy and students for the clergy were excluded from the obligation to serve even beyond their student days. Yet I watched with horror as so many young people my age struggled with their response to being drafted. In fact, on March 5, 1969, I recall vividly taking part in a daylong vigil in the chapel of the Jewish Theological Seminary to support one young man, Burton Freed, who refused to be drafted due to his opposition to the war. Surrounded by others, he awaited the arrival of federal marshals who would take him into custody. Rabbi Heschel spoke to us during that emotional day. I especially remember his haunting melody for peace, "Oseh Shalom Bimromav" "May the One Who makes peace in the Heavens make peace for us", which he taught us that day. It was one of his own compositions. That melody remains with me to this day. I love to teach it to others. I taught it in Vietnam without sharing the dramatic circumstances in which I first heard it.

While clergy students of all faiths were protected from the draft, the U.S. military needed chaplains to voluntarily enlist. For the Jewish community, the National Jewish Welfare Board was the liaison to the government and was given a quota of chaplains needed. In turn, representatives of that agency appealed to students to consider choosing to serve. There was a major shortfall in meeting the quota especially among rabbis. During my tour in Vietnam, we were visited by the Army's Chief of Chaplains, Chaplain (General) Sampson. An aide told me that at year's end 14 rabbis would be separating from service, and only 6 would be entering, leaving 21 in all.

I recall feeling guilt over my privileged position. I could freely choose my path forward while so many others could not. I was sympathetic to the need for the presence of rabbis especially under such trying circumstances. The commitment would be limited to two years and the likelihood of being deployed to Vietnam was remote although possible. My twin brother Sherwin had completed his service as a Flight Surgeon in the U.S. Air Force, and I knew that his experience as a young flight surgeon had been positive.

I struggled mightily with my decision. I did not want to be identified with support of the war to which wearing a uniform would surely testify. I did not want to surrender my ability to speak out against the war. Yet how could I not feel responsible for brethren who were drafted? I took part in endless conversations with fellow students, friends, family, staff, and faculty at the Seminary. In retrospect, I wish I had gone to my teacher, Rabbi Heschel, for counsel. In the end, it was a very personal and lonely choice. After much heart searching, I decided to step forward and to accept a commission in the U.S. Army.

# 2 Entering Service

I had a rude awakening on my first day while undergoing my induction physical in Brooklyn in June, 1969. At one point, I was asked to produce a urine specimen. While standing at the urinal, a young man standing next to me whispered urgently: "Share and share alike."

I was stunned and completely taken aback, not comprehending what he meant. I probably treated him badly by not responding at all. In retrospect, I surmised that there was something likely to be discovered in his own urine sample that would bar his way into the Army. He hoped that mine would help him evade detection. He wanted to enlist! Service in the Army might have been a way for him to climb out of poverty and to make something of his life. Others were fleeing, but he wanted to be in!

Chaplain School at Fort Hamilton in Brooklyn was essentially a rapid introduction to military culture. We learned how to wear our uniforms properly, how the army was organized into units, about the chain of command. We practiced responding to commands and marching in formation. We took part in daily physical training, modified greatly from the rigors faced by most recruits. We spent one week at Fort Dix in New Jersey for at least a glimpse of a more demanding regimen. I was pressed up against my own limits when we ran through an obstacle course and crawled on our bellies across a field with live machine gun fire overhead. I remember with some shame how I was immobilized with my arm and leg muscles in spasm when trying to climb a rope ladder over a wall. An empathetic drill sergeant said quietly: "It's OK, chaplain. Relax. You can come down now."

During this brief six-week period, I had a glimpse of one remarkable feature of military life. My roommate was a young man from the Church of Christ. Christian and Jewish clergy (there were no Muslim chaplains at that period) were roommates, shared everything, and became fast friends. I would later experience how close the interfaith bonds would be among us. Mutual support and curiosity about each other within the military would be hard to replicate in civilian settings.

# CHAPTER 3

# Fort Lewis

*With Mark Gumbiner, preparing for Passover at Fort Lewis*

At Fort Lewis near Tacoma, Washington, I began my service as a Jewish Chaplain. It was a major training post for new recruits, and it was also an embarkation gateway to Vietnam. Troops trained elsewhere often passed through on their way to the war zone. Our Jewish Chapel in a visible central part of the fort overflowed with Jews. With my able assistant, Mark Gumbiner, we tried in every conceivable way to create opportunities for being together and sharing our hopes and our sorrows.

There were lighter moments among the more somber. I arrived shortly before the Jewish High Holy Days, and we offered a full range of services along with social time and plenty of strictly kosher meals and snacks. There were ample provisions for those who observed the dietary laws.

On Kol Nidre night, the dramatic beginning of Yom Kippur, when our one Torah scroll was removed from the Holy Ark, I asked my assistant to find a volunteer who would be honored to hold the scroll before the congregation. He disappeared into the crowd, and soon a soldier with a buzz cut ascended the pulpit. Someone slipped a kippah onto his head and a tallit around his shoulders. I handed him the Torah and directed him to face the congregation. He fulfilled his responsibility faithfully and then descended into the crowd. We learned afterwards that he was attracted to the crowd at the entrance to the chapel and walked over to investigate. Suddenly he was approached randomly and invited up to the pulpit. In the army, one is expected to follow directions. He was not Jewish! I often wondered how he processed this experience on the most sacred night of the Jewish year and how he shared it with his own family and friends.

I soon learned painfully how simply wearing a uniform exposed one to derision and humiliation. Soon after arriving at my post, I contacted rabbinic colleagues in the area who welcomed me warmly. At one point, I made my way to the Hillel House at the University of Washington to meet with its distinguished director, Rabbi Arthur Jacobovitz. Approaching the entrance, I was confronted by several students. I was in uniform, and they could see from my insignia that I was a chaplain. There was no opportunity for conversation. I was immediately assaulted verbally: "How can you be a man of God and still get out there and teach 'Kill! Kill! Kill?!'"

I was totally unprepared and stunned into silence. There was no chance to enter dialogue. There was no opportunity to explain that I, too, opposed this war. Dressed as a soldier, I represented the warmakers. I wanted to sink into the earth and to disappear. Whatever was my personal purpose in uniform, to many I was looked upon as complicit in an immoral foreign war. I quickly entered the building to escape the encounter.

Entering the Army and its rigid chain of command, I knew theoretically that these two years would be a time of silence for me whatever misgivings I had about the present mission of the military. I would soon learn the price if I even appeared to step over a certain line. On October 14, 1969, Moratorium Day was declared. It was to be set aside as a day when Americans would

*Speaking to rabbincal students in New York*

gather to take stock of the war in Vietnam. All views were to be aired. My understanding was that it was not a day for protest but of honest conversation.

Out of uniform, I decided to attend a rabbinic meeting in Seattle on Moratorium Day mostly to listen. We were all asked to sign a letter supporting the goals of the day. I decided to sign the letter, and it appeared the next day in a Seattle newspaper. I was not identified as a military chaplain. The following day I was summoned to a meeting with the post chaplain, a Catholic priest devoting his career to the Army. I was scolded for attending the Moratorium Day event, and I was warned that I should never do such a thing again. I learned there would be little patience with even the appearance of public dissent while I was in service.

Even within the fort, I came into close contact with the tensions around the war. Among my duties was to visit the stockade where men were imprisoned for a wide variety of infractions. My role was to mingle among those who were confined to offer a listening pastoral ear and to discover if there was anything I might do to counsel or to help. I quickly found that among those incarcerated were some thoughtful and admirable people who had refused their orders to Vietnam or others who had initiated applications for Conscientious Objector status after entering active duty. I remember one man who, while facing a four-year sentence for refusing to go overseas, was one of the happiest men alive. He had finally spoken the truth his conscience dictated. While there was little concretely I could do for him or others as they awaited disposition of their cases, I could affirm them by listening intensely as they poured out their hearts.

Six months after beginning my service, I was invited back to the Seminary to address the student body about the chaplaincy. Debate about the military chaplaincy had not abated. I readily acknowledged that compromise, holding back, and not being wholly myself were inevitably part of being a chaplain in this moment. Yet I argued as cogently as I could for the importance of the presence of rabbis in uniform. Anticipating my upcoming meeting with rabbinical students, I invited a focus group of young men active in our Jewish program to learn what they would say regarding the value of rabbis in uniform. Here is one response:

*I am a college graduate; I have spent 1 ½ years in Vista and was drafted at the age of 24.*

*There is a world you can't see or would like to believe does not exist, that of an enlisted man . . . We exist at the bottom of the totem pole, and, because of it, the buck stops with me. The oppressiveness of the military system is one of depersonalization and repetition. We are not individuals but ranks. We hold no truths or are allowed to tell them to anyone because we only exist for the whim of the command. Be it, we accept our position and suffer through two years of this oppressive life of repetition.*

*Personal problems abound, and with Jewish personnel they are multiplied. There are far too few Jewish Chaplains in the Army for the problems of the enlisted Jewish personnel. The need for helping us is urgent.*

*For no matter what you feel on the War and the morality of it, there are Jewish personnel in the Army who have problems and are suffering. No matter what compromises you rationalize for not putting in two years for us, there are Jewish personnel in the Army who are suffering. The problems are there, and Jewish personnel seek your help because if you shrink your duty as a Rabbi in not compromising your principles for the benefit of your fellow Jew, there are Jewish personnel in the Army who are suffering.*

I shared that cogent expression of need, and then described some of my own intense experiences with people in uniform even in the short period I had served:

*There's Mike, a college man who came to know himself as he went through his training and found that he could not ever be a party to violence. He filed as a CO, was turned down, and refused an order to go to Vietnam. Facing up to five years in prison, he went to trial, and he comes to you to stand as a witness on his behalf. In one of my happiest moments in the Army, I saw his case dismissed because he wasn't accorded due process of law. He now is applying again as a CO.*

*There is Mark, a man who was decorated as a helicopter gunner in Vietnam, yet progressively has found the authority in the Army intolerable. After taking every kind of drug available, disobeying orders, escaping from a stockade in Vietnam only to be apprehended in Hawaii, spending a year imprisoned at Leavenworth, and going AWOL at every possible moment, he comes to you for help in finding a way out.*

*There is Arnold who calls you frantically one night because he fears he will be forced to ship overseas. He has made no friends. While on leave, he was enticed to a party, and he has no recollection of the last two weeks. He wants to see a psychiatrist, but no one will listen to him.*

*There is Felix, a most unusual Jewish boy who grew up on a farm and spent the last few years as a rider on the rodeo circuit. He is terribly quiet, but you discover that deep within he is seriously contemplating*

*Teaching at Fort Lewis*

*suicide because he cannot communicate with his fellow soldiers nor tolerate the rigorous discipline. He is suffering from physical pain constantly because of earlier injuries, but he has not received attention. From his enclosed self, he looks out helplessly and alone, unable to reach out to call for help.*

*You would meet John, an amazingly sensitive young man who feels he has grown up in the Army as a medic and civil affairs officer in Vietnam. But he has come back and been placed in a position where he has nothing more than menial, time passing duties which have reduced him to a state of almost uncontrolled anger. He comes to you to ask for your help in getting a transfer to a post where he can do some useful work and go on with his studies.*

*There is Marv who sits in your office and has flashbacks right before your eyes. He is to be shipped to Vietnam, and he is in such a state of mental anguish over the thought that he is almost beyond the realm of being reached. He started taking drugs while in the Army, and now hates the Army venomously. He can't face the prospect of going to Vietnam.*

*There is Dick who calls you one night with a bullet hole in his foot and who pleads with you to keep him from being shipped out in the morning without medical attention, John who pleads with you in the stockade to see if you can hasten his discharge so that he can return home to try to save a crumbling marriage, Jack, on orders for Vietnam, who wants help to obtain a discharge because he is an only son whose father and mother are unable to work and are about to go on welfare.*

21

During my relatively short time as a chaplain, I had discovered how much I was needed. I had no regrets about my decision.

Surely one of the best gifts that my time of service bestowed on me was finding the woman who would become my wife. I was single and unattached when leaving the Seminary, and I was lonely. Recognizing my need, my rabbinic colleagues immediately set to work. When introducing me to a young woman, Lorri Grashin, Rabbi Moshe Pomerance declared: "This is not a date." This is a "shidduch" (a match!). Within five months, we were engaged.

My future in-laws, Arthur and Beverly Grashin, were ambivalent about this match because of their own personal history. They had married in 1943. They had hours together before he was shipped off to Europe where, as an infantryman, he participated in the Battle of the Bulge. They did not see each other for three years. Now their daughter was committed to another man in uniform during another war.

While we had planned for a summer wedding, our plans were upended when I received orders to Vietnam effective in June. We had to decide quickly whether to push up our wedding date or to wait upon my return. We were in turmoil.

Lorri's parents counseled us to wait. My future mother-in-law quipped, however, that, were we not yet married, she would accompany her daughter as a chaperone if we wanted to meet in Hawaii during my tour!

We were clear that we wanted to be married before my departure date. Our families made our wish come true. Our wedding took place in Seattle in the presence of family, dear friends and colleagues, and many new friends from my congregation at Fort Lewis. We would have almost a month together.

In preparation for signing out at Fort Lewis, I underwent two days of training specifically for those about to be deployed to Vietnam. I remember the darkened theatre setting in which films were screened warning us of the dangers of sexually transmitted diseases which were epidemic and dangerous drugs which were cheap and possibly lethal. We were led through a day of field training where a forest became the scene of simulated jungle combat complete with U.S. soldiers acting as the enemy. The training seemed generic for everyone about to go to Vietnam. I had no focused guidance about serving as a chaplain, certainly not as a chaplain serving Jews.

# CHAPTER 4

# Arrival in Vietnam

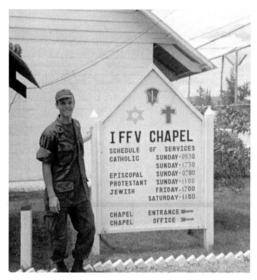

*In front of interfaith chapel, Nha Trang*

It was excruciating to leave my wife so soon after our marriage. While I missed her terribly every day of our separation, she provided a lifeline for me, knowing that someone so special awaited my return. Practically her presence in my life enabled me to write this account fifty years later. Our letters and audio tapes provided a careful record of my daily journeys and encounters.

Another source of great comfort during this war was the blessing of telephone connections from time to time. A network of volunteer amateur radio operators in the States provided inexpensive though awkward opportunities to be in touch with loved ones in real time. Our cost was the rate of the telephone connection from the operator's home to our loved ones.

We learned to ignore the fact that the operator was listening and to say "over" when we wanted to hear each other's voice. Since letters and audio tapes would bring dated news from the time of mailing, speaking and listening in real time made a big difference. While the network often was unavailable or broken down, hearing the voice of my wife even while we were oceans apart could raise my spirits totally. While we never met the individuals who generously gave of themselves to enable our contacts, we are forever in their debt. We used more expensive conventional phone lines sparingly.

Another unusual benefit of deployment to Vietnam was the date we were given for our return home and separation from service. It was called our DEROS, date of estimated return from overseas. The duration of the tour was one full year. Virtually all the people I knew relished being able to immediately count down days until the end of their tour especially when becoming a "double digit midget" with under 100 days to go or experiencing the joys of being a "short timer" when the end was in sight. How much time left in our tour of duty was part of every dialogue.

The other potent energizer was the prospect of R & R, a six-day rest and recuperation period, and a two week leave that was implemented during my tour of service. Planning for these times of reunion and relief from the war zone was a constant source of anticipation and conversation. These times away provided oases of comfort.

# 5 My Assignment

CHAPTER

My assignment was to care for the spiritual needs of Jews in II Corps, a sweeping area in the Central Highlands of South Vietnam encompassing

26

almost 50% of the country. My predecessor had departed months before my arrival. I had rabbinic colleagues to the north, Bob Krause, and to the south, Fred Wenger, both frequent collaborators and constant sources of support. We had entered the Army and trained together, and we all arrived in Vietnam at the same time. Fred and I were seated together on the long flight from Travis Air Force Base. His companionship eased my loneliness and apprehension considerably. Rabbi Sandy Dresin was also serving in the South. A career chaplain, he was completing a tour that would end in November. His experience helped orient us newcomers and bolstered our confidence.

My office was at II Corps Headquarters in Nha Trang on the coast of the South China Sea, a picturesque setting which masked the reality of wartime. Across the street from our office was a pristine beach with white sand above which lofty coconut palms swayed with the breeze. On that beach, one could always purchase fresh pineapple, coconut, and dragon fruit. The water was the temperature of a warm bath. Within a few days of my arrival, I crossed the street to the beach. I wrote to my wife:

*Today I took my first step in the local economy. I went down to the beach after lunch to purchase a pineapple. I found a lady named "Nam," an older lady with a big straw oriental hat and two baskets of fruit suspended from each end of a stick which she carries across her shoulders. She has pineapples, coconuts, peanuts, and bananas. She offered one to me for 100 piasters, and I bargained her down to 80 as I was instructed to do. It was really fun to play the game which everyone does – and the pineapple was delicious. I've even learned a few words of Vietnamese already.*

Nha Trang was a poor town. Its modest landscape was dominated by a large pure white Buddha set on an elevated platform. Any flight into Nha Trang had an impressive view of the Buddha.

My office also housed the Protestant Staff Chaplain, (Col) Joe Andrews, a Catholic Asst. Staff Chaplain, (LtC) Ford and later Chaplain (LtC) Wetzel,

*Prominent Buddha in Nha Trang*

and staff to support our work. Adjacent to our office was a non-denominational chapel in which all our services were held. In the most imposing building in our compound, once a fashionable French era hotel, the commanding general for II Corps and his staff had their offices.

My living quarters were in another old French hotel that had known much better days. I shared my room with large cockroaches which were pursued relentlessly by lizards. Yet it was mine alone with a private bath, a refuge for me after the often-trying events of the day.

I was informed that there were an estimated 500 Jewish personnel scattered widely across my region. My responsibility included Jews serving in all branches of the military primarily Army and Air Force. Most were in established rear bases. Others would be found widely scattered in units and compounds often with perhaps one or two Jews. In the large, well established bases, we often had ongoing programs with lay leadership which we tried earnestly to support.

In Pleiku, I soon met one exceptional lay leader who deeply impressed me. I wrote about his influence to my wife:

*My host, Dr. Albie Hornblass, is an ophthalmic surgeon and has been here almost eleven months. He has been the lay leader, and you can't imagine what he has been able to do. It's a small group – about fifteen or so – but they have a great feeling of camaraderie . . . Albie has a yeshiva background. In*

28

*fact, he was president of the student body at Yeshiva University, active in United Jewish Appeal (UJA), and just has tremendous commitment. He goes out of his way for the Jewish guys in a big way.*

Volunteer lay leaders were precious, but we struggled mightily as lay leaders moved to other units or came to the end of their tours. We constantly seemed to be in search of new replacements.

I would endeavor to visit each of these centers monthly if possible. I was fortunate that I was preceded by rabbis and their assistants who had worked hard to establish Jewish programming wherever possible. Our task was to build upon these existing programs.

I was not working alone. I was blessed with two able assistants, Bob Elson and Ed Finkelstein, both hard working and dedicated to our mission. They routinely traveled with me, helping me carry the substantial supplies (mostly food!) we delivered to every program. They were also charged with protecting me, and they were always armed with M16s. I deeply valued my non-combatant status. I was never armed. In fact, I was determined never even to touch a weapon during my two years of service. While training at Fort Dix, chaplains were given the options of weapon training, and of assembling, cleaning, and disassembling M16s. I elected to skip the training.

The distances between major bases were substantial, accessible mainly by air. I knew that my life would be largely spent traveling aboard innumerable varieties of aircraft from helicopters of every sort to troop carriers,

*Ed Finkelstein with supplies for a journey*

even to the occasional Lear jet on which I hitched a ride with a general officer or a colonel.

Here is a typical monthly schedule, from August 1970:

| 4 | August | Dalat | Weekday Service |
|---|---|---|---|
| 7-8 | August | Pleiku | Sabbath services |
| 9 | August | Kontum | Weekday Service |
| 11 | August | Nha Trang | Tishah B'Av |
| 12 | August | Tuy Hoa | Weekday Service |
| 14-15 | August | Cam Ranh Bay | Sabbath Services |
| 17 | August | LZ English | Weekday Service |
| 18-20 | August | Nha Trang | Lay leadership Conference |
| 21-22 | August | Phan Rang | Sabbath Services |
| 25 | August | Song Mao | Weekday Service |
| 26 | August | Phan Thiet | Weekday Service |
| 28-29 | August | Qui Nhon | Sabbath Services |
| 30 | August | Phu Cat | Weekday Service |

# 6 Building Sanctuaries in Time

*High Holiday Sanctuary in Cam Rahn Bay*

I discovered immediately that time in the war zone was distinctly different than back in the "world", a common expression pointing to the distance between our present reality and the beloved land from which we had come. Time was not differentiated. Every day was a workday, not dissimilar from the day before and the day after. There were no days off. It was at times a challenge to name the day of the week.

In contrast, Jewish tradition has a sophisticated toolbox for shaping time into sanctuaries, each with its own unique potential for holiness. My purpose was to help relieve the grating monotony of time by bringing at least a taste of the sacred days in the Jewish calendar. I wanted to provide at least a reminder of the familiar round of special times. Liturgy, melodies, rituals, words of Torah, and, most especially, food could awaken memories and provide comfort.

Having mentioned the food that we carried, I hasten to add that we could not find most of what we wanted to serve at a military commissary or on the local market. Instead, we were always well supplied with kosher food from the National Jewish Welfare Board. Our responsibility included providing kosher food regularly to any personnel who observed Kashrut, and we also had ample remaining provisions to set the table with kosher choices at virtually all our programs. The staples from the JWB included quantities of Hebrew National canned braised beef with rice, meat balls, and stuffed cabbage, bottled gefilte fish and horseradish, and kosher wine. When the High Holidays and Passover drew near and we were able to bring large numbers together, the JWB provided for us handsomely.

My office often overflowed with supplements to JWB shipments. I cannot recount how many packages we received from caring Jewish veterans' organizations, women's auxiliaries, synagogue sisterhoods, youth groups, and our own families. Kosher salamis were popular gifts. Those that arrived after long journeys at sea were often coated with green mold, but we never tired of trimming away the unwanted parts to salvage the tasty central core.

Of course, Jewish personnel in Vietnam represented the same spectrum of knowledge and commitment as Jews back home. There were learned and committed Orthodox, Conservative, and Reform Jews, and many with little or no background at all. Of necessity, every gathering was planned for a wide variety of needs. We did not have the luxury to organize multiple offerings to meet that wider spectrum. We could offer one place and one activity with a wide embrace.

I came to revere the prayer books and Bibles published by the National Jewish Welfare Board. They are the heroic product of a panel of rabbis from all the major movements. Each one had to compromise to create a place where everyone could stand. Among the troops I served, I do not recall even one Orthodox Jew complaining that the service was too adulterated for his needs, nor do I recollect even one more liberal soldier lamenting that the service was too traditional for her. As a rabbi, I was welcomed without anyone asserting that my personal orientation was unsuited for him or her. Everyone wanted to stand together and so made room for every other.

## WEEKDAYS

Wherever I traveled on weekdays, I carried a chaplain's field kit which included prayer books, a miniature printed scroll of Torah, a Kiddush cup, candle holders and more. The container for the kit could function as a small Ark to contain the Torah. We would generally begin with a service conducted wherever we could. At times it took place in the bush or on a firebase carved out at the top of a hill. More often than not we did not have a minyan of ten Jews, at times just one or two; but frequently others in the vicinity would gather to see what was happening. Everyone was welcomed.

I soon realized that the brief prayer service served as a pretext for the main event, an opportunity to gather and to be fully present with one another. Invariably, some simple snacks were offered. At times we filled cups with Shapiro's Concord Wine to offer a L'Chayim. The wine was awful, but the moment set apart from daily chores was appreciated. Conversations might begin with small talk but soon might touch on serious personal issues and feelings and the need for advice or intervention. With time being short, and these meetings only occurring infrequently, we had incentives to reach the nub of the issue quickly. Those personal meetings between strangers proved to be among the most satisfying experiences for me when I felt most needed.

My visits were always announced and coordinated in advance. I quickly found that I was warmly welcomed uniformly even beyond the Jewish personnel. Song Mao was among the most desolate posts on my itinerary. I described my experience to my wife:

*Of all the places I have gone, this place has impressed me because of the geniality of the men. When I've come, everyone seems to expect me and knows who I am. The commanding officer gives us his own room for our meeting and always asks me in just to chat and to check that all my needs are met. When I consider that there are only 4 Jews out of 1016 men here, I am really impressed. Maybe it's because they have no resident chaplain here at all. A priest and a minister visit on Sundays for services.*

I admit my frustration that meetings were fleeting and infrequent due to the size of the region. In addition, personnel changed so quickly as tours ended or units were transferred from place to place. I longed for more continuity and regularity so that trust and friendship could be nurtured. I had to learn to accept a less satisfying reality.

Encouraging regular Torah study was an aspiration which I carried. Was I delighted when I found that there was a receptive audience. We established regular classes first in Nha Trang and then in Cam Ranh Bay where we studied prayer, ethics, and upcoming holiday rituals. I knew that Jewish learning could be a balm and a source of uplift. Discussion was frequent and vigorous.

I carried a selection of sacred books both for personal learning and to share with others. I soon found that the tropical climate with its monsoons and high humidity took its toll on book bindings. Some of my books were unusable by the end of my tour. Yet it was unthinkable to be without at least a modest library of holy books.

Weekday travels at times could bring a surprise. On a visit to An Khe in March, I had such a moment. After a visit with the only Jew in the encampment, I wrote:

*The chaplain up there, a friendly guy, took me around to meet some of the command. As I reached out to shake hands with the colonel who is the commander, he began to talk to me in Hebrew! I was astounded! He was a military attaché in Tel Aviv from 1964-66, and he thinks so much of the land. We talked and shared experiences. A warm guy and obviously sharp. For a few minutes while we were together I completely forgot where we were and the usual stiff politeness used when talking with higher officers. Such a pleasure. His name is Col. Read.*

## SHABBAT

As in Jewish life anywhere in the world, Shabbat was the hub of programming in Vietnam as well. We tried very hard to make certain that a Shabbat program took place weekly in every major base organized by willing lay leaders. I would rotate through Cam Ranh Bay, Pleiku, An Khe, Qui Nhon, Phan Rang, Phu Cat, and Nha Trang for Shabbat on a regular basis. The focus would be on Friday evening when many were free, but we tried to offer Shabbat morning services, too, whenever possible even if the numbers would be smaller.

It was on these occasions that we came closest to developing a meaningful sense of community. Every familiar melody, each reading in Hebrew or English that resonated with memory, each exchange of simple 'Shabbat Shalom' greetings, helped transform and lift that time into another welcome zone. Conversations over kiddush were often the most important segment of the program.

What we served on each occasion was quite different from the mess hall's menu. I recall once packing a Shabbat dinner for Phu Cat, a prominent Air Force base. The menu included local rolls made from rice flour, meat balls (from Hebrew National cans), watermelon, gefilte fish, and horseradish. One special kiddush treat involved lining up a row of meatballs along a sliced rice roll, an Ed Finkelstein creation! Our original "meatball hoagie"! This was our Shabbat meal! The offerings were not elegant, but they awakened latent memories of home.

I recall with gratitude occasional Sabbaths spent with men who relished a more full-bodied day of rest. I especially have in mind Drs. Joshua Sternberg and Steve Stein in Qui Nhon, Dr. Albie Hornblass in Pleiku, and Dr. Dave Berris in An Khe.

In Qui Nhon, I sat down with Josh, Steve, and a few others to a Shabbat dinner complete with Kiddush, stuffed cabbage, a delicious homemade kugel made with noodles, peaches, apples, raisins, and cinnamon, gefilte fish, rolls, and salad. We sang z'mirot, Shabbat table songs, talked endlessly, and concluded with birchat HaMazon, the prayer of thanksgiving after the meal. Shabbat morning was spent in prayer with a smaller group, and Shabbat afternoon often included studying with Josh, singing more of our favorite z'mirot, and a welcome nap before the havdalah ritual separating Shabbat from the week to come. In the company of these men, we entered an island of the familiar amidst the chaos of war.

I tried hard to share short, informal messages during our services that were keyed to our troubled present situation. One Shabbat in Pleiku:

*I talked about how extraordinary it is when the values of the environment are overcome and a man rises above them even in an atmosphere where his own values might seem so out of place. Values like the preciousness of life, concern for each other, living in a distinctive, Jewish way, caring for Israel.*

There were times when the tranquility we tried to summon was broken by the reality in which we lived. During one Friday evening service at Phan Rang, an Air Force base, a siren sounded when a mortar attack occurred. The service ended abruptly. Every person in the chapel where we assembled knew his role in the event of an emergency and swiftly ran to his post. I stood motionlessly until I was literally tackled by one of the men, reminding me to stay prone until the all-clear was sounded. There was no way to complete that service.

It wouldn't be the only time I was obliged to hit the ground when mortar shells fell. While visiting Landing Zone English, I was taking an outdoor shower when the sirens sounded. Everyone was instructed to lie low near sandbags that were omnipresent. I complied in my birthday suit, and no one else even seemed to notice. Life threatening situations overshadowed any consideration of personal modesty.

Shabbat, the gem of our tradition, could be one of the loneliest days for me when I was not involved in a service. It was a normal workday for everyone else, and it was especially painful when I had no choice but to spend long hours alone. My books for study and prayer were my lifelines.

I made a point of composing a new prayer for peace for every Shabbat service. Here is one sample:

*Shalom. What beauty there can be in a word, in the images it evokes, in the hope it nourishes, in the light it radiates. Shalom is from the root "shalem." It means complete, whole. O God, how incomplete we are without peace. How we long to be whole again. A world without peace is a world stunted, unfinished. Help us to find shalom – here, among all nations, among all men.*

Here is one more:

*Our God,*

*Grant us peace, Your most precious gift, You, the eternal source of peace, enable us to be its messenger throughout the world. Bless this land that it may soon be a stronghold of peace, that war which has so long plagued and distorted the lives of its people will soon be only a painful memory. May contentment reign within its borders, health and happiness within its homes. Strengthen the bonds of friendship and fellowship among the inhabitants of all lands. Plant virtue in every soul and help each of us to become the building blocks for peace in the way we live and speak and think. Grant that we never become accustomed to the absence of peace, that we never tire of its quest, that we long and work for its blessings with every fiber of our being.*

## TISHAH B'AV

Having arrived during the summer, the first special day of note was the fast of the Ninth of Av. While it was not the time I would have chosen to become more acquainted with members of my widely scattered congregation, we were eager to make the full panoply of the Jewish calendar come alive even in this unlikely setting. Our office published a monthly bulletin which we distributed across our region. I wrote my first bulletin message after having made my rounds for the first time to meet everyone in person.

*I have been astonished to find real small but vibrant communities.*

*As you know, the Jewish calendar contains in its round an expression of every mood and emotion. The joyful and the ecstatic are counterpointed by the solemn and the tragic. During the month of Av which we are entering, the low is reached when we observe Tishah B'Av. It is a day of fasting and mourning for the tragedies which have devastated our people repeatedly over the centuries . . . No doubt the consciousness of these tragedies is sobering, even traumatic. Yet it also has the effect of heightening our awareness of the miracle of our survival as Jews. We learn first-hand the scope and depth of the sacrifices which our brethren have made to preserve our heritage for us. We begin to experience the need to treasure and become part of that heritage ourselves. The day is not pleasant; perhaps it is even painful, but the history of our people is so stamped with blood and tears that we as Jews can never hope to know ourselves until we have faced this tragic truth.*

*In many of your areas, special Tishah B'Av services will be held.*

On the evening of August 10 in Nha Trang, a group of us sat on the ground in candlelight to recite the Biblical book of Lamentations, an extended elegy over the destruction of Jerusalem and the suffering of its inhabitants. Even in this unlikely setting, we were determined to express our connectedness to Jewish history.

No one could come together in the morning, so it was a solitary day for me. After prayers, I busied myself planning for the lay leaders' conference which was scheduled for the next week. I broke the fast with a peppered beef sandwich on Vietnamese bread with mustard, pickle, and a coke. The beef came vacuum packed from my wife. It was surely not a typical break-the-fast meal, but little would be "usual" in this setting.

38

## ROSH HASHANAH AND YOM KIPPUR

While normally it was incumbent on me and my assistant to go out to connect with troops wherever they were stationed, there were some precious times when it was possible to gather many together. The High Holidays were one of those times. We worked feverishly in preparation for the holidays. We made certain that command letters were prepared and disbursed allowing temporary leave to meet religious obligations. We often worked with Christian chaplains around our region to make certain that everyone knew of our plans and was encouraged to attend. The chaplains were very attentive to Jewish needs.

Lay leaders were a keystone in our far-flung program. Twice during my tour, we arranged lay leadership conferences in Nha Trang, before the High Holy Days and again before Passover. In each case, we brought our volunteers together for an intensive day of learning and fellowship. I joked with my wife about adding her to the schedule as a guest speaker:

*I've included your name. Your session will be entitled: "How we can all get out of Vietnam quickly so that we can go home and have women around because women are necessary for Jewish life!"*

In mid-August, about fifteen of us spent the day together. We studied together, brainstormed for ideas to engage our fellow Jews, and built friendships with one another. I reported to my wife:

*The conference went very smoothly. It was relaxed but businesslike, and we got everything done I had hoped. Started with a Shacharit service at 8:30, then coffee and mom's brownies. I saved them because they were so perfect. Then a welcome by me and by Father Ford, the Deputy Staff Chaplain, and to work. We talked about the Holidays, arrangements, parts in the service, preparing for Yom Tov. Then two hours for lunch. Some took in the beach. In the afternoon, we talked about supplies, problems in the congregations, and lots of ideas for programming – even a movie about the High Holy Days. We finished at 4:00 and had a break until 5:30 when we all had dinner together. We had salad, baked potatoes, mixture of Hebrew National meats, and cokes.*

Of course, we hoped that each leader would encourage everyone to join us when we all came together for the Holidays.

After the conference, some of our lay leaders were able to stay for a day or two to enjoy the amenities of Nha Trang. Among the special attractions was a visit from Miss America and her entourage to help raise morale. They arrived at our compound and entertained at a show in the evening. I learned later that a caged monkey in our compound reached out and managed to grasp Miss America's hair as she passed by, pulling her against the cage! Fortunately, she was quickly freed without injury!

We decided on Cam Ranh Bay as the site for our services and gatherings. Facilities included an air-conditioned chapel and dining area, and ample barracks for housing. Beyond services, we sought good opportunities for rest, recreation, and being together. The nearby beach proved especially popular.

High Holiday services require special skill sets for cantors, Torah readers, and shofar blowers. While I was prepared to take on the bulk of responsibilities personally, I was surprised and delighted to find able volunteers. David Berris from An Khe, Steve Stein from Qui Nhon, Al Belsky from Phan Rang, and Joel Brauner from Nha Trang stepped forward to lead. I could concentrate on holding everything together and writing messages that I hoped would comfort and uplift.

I did not expect that I would become a TV producer and director among my chaplaincy roles. Yet on an island off the coast of Nha Trang, Hon Tri, there was a TV studio programming for the GIs. Religiously themed programs were encouraged as well. Before Rosh HaShanah, I traveled by helicopter to the island, a script and props in hand. Of course, I brought with me a shofar, the ram's horn, that ancient instrument whose sound captures the essence of the season. I recounted the experience of creating a TV program:

*We recorded the program three times – there were a number of video mechanical mishaps – but I was much more composed than I thought I would be. Looking at one camera and then, by signal, at another, trying to remember by heart as much of the talk as possible, and worrying how the shofar would sound, made me a little nervous. But I was pretty cool about it all. They made two good video tapes and are going to try to get them around to all the stations before Yomtov.*

The program focused on the shofar. Following is part of the message that was recorded:

*The sounds (of the shofar) are similar to moaning and crying, rabbinic tradition tells us. They are deeply human sounds of misery and frustration. Especially do they represent the sounds of a person who has probed one's own shortcomings and is striving to repent. The very shape of the shofar itself resembles a contrite person – bent over in one's sorrow and humility... The shofar blast humbles us, adjuring us to take on the shape and the sound of the instrument itself.*

*Yet there is a second message, one which exalts and strengthens the back which has been bent over in contrition. In days past, the shofar was used to proclaim the freeing of slaves, and today the sound still carries a triumphant message concerning human freedom. Outer freedom from chains and masters, certainly. Inner freedom, too, the ability to remake our lives and to reform the world. The shofar reminds us that we need never be petrified. Our lives can ever be vessels of youth which are subject to our molding again and again. One of the essential, unique qualities of being human is one's ability to do teshuvah, to genuinely repent and change one's ways. One can recast the way one deals with others, one's patterns of thought and speech, one's relationship with God. And in the world at large, one can with others do something to remove some of those scourges which disrupt our lives and disturb our peace, tragedies of human hunger, of families without homes, of young lives cut off or maimed long before their maturity, of war.*

*These High Holidays are difficult and demanding times for a Jew. One is, by turns, lowered and raised, humbled, then exalted. Yet, as the day-long fast of Yom Kippur ends, the worshippers emerge uplifted and with inspired hope as they listen to the last long triumphant blast of the shofar.*

That poignant sound of the shofar was broadcast all over Vietnam. My hope was that it would penetrate even to those who could not join us in Cam Ranh Bay.

As Rosh Hashanah approached, our anxiety grew. We had worked so diligently to create a meaningful experience for everyone who would come. I recall the excitement of the men and a few women arriving. The women served as nurses or worked at the USO. I had met many in my travels, but there were some new faces, too. The anticipation and joy of this reprieve were palpable.

Knowing that the meals served would be indispensable to providing a memorable experience, we collaborated with the mess sergeant to plan the menus. We kashered a big 10 gallon cauldron and needed utensils to make soup. Kosher TV dinners with disposable tableware were at the center. Everyone seemed content.

I tried hard to speak to the situation in which all of us found ourselves. On the first day of Rosh Hashanah, I looked out at my special congregation and said:

*Whatever each of us present feels about the war, about our presence here, I don't think any of us can help becoming changed. Transported far from everything which was familiar to us and from all those we love, each of those things and people suddenly become larger than life. Whereas before we may have lived among them almost without noticing, suddenly we are more sensitive in their absence. We think more about a mother and father, about a wife or husband, a close friend, about home, a chance to study in school, a day of leisure in the country, even a warm shower and a flush toilet. We make promises how we'll never take them for granted again, how we'll treasure them.*

*And among those things which we learn so much to love is peace. I don't think that we can ever look upon that word again without a deeply personal feeling of attachment. It will jump out at us from every written page. The subject is no longer distant or theoretical . . . War and peace really are our lives this year, and now the difference between them really stands out.*

I simply felt compelled at that moment to speak about peace. I went on to outline the central place that peace occupies among Jewish values, how it is the necessary "vessel that contains every other blessing".

*In fact, it seems that for the fulfillment of all our greatest dreams, peace must be present. To be with the ones we love, to raise children into a healthy world, to write a poem or a book, to build a home or nation, to worship God, to dream clearly of a better world, and to act upon that dream, we are in desperate need of peace. Amidst the uncertainties and sounds of war, it's so hard to create, to write, to think, to pray, to love, even to breathe deeply.*

*Yet here we are in the midst of war. That is a reality, and we cannot wish it away... Yet we must guard ourselves from ever being comfortable with war and from forgetting to dream of peace. We must never lose the sense of the absurdity of war, of the distortions that it forces on human lives. The thought of human beings hunting one another. The thought of one man putting an end to the life of another, the thought of people working to create more destructive weapons for war must stir up in us a feeling of horror. When we accept overkill, huge arsenals, body counts . . . , we have ceased to be human. We've lost the image of God in which we were created.*

I then asked if there was anything we could do even during war to change our reality.

*I feel there is – within our own lives – in the circle of people in which we function. We can be peaceful people. Despite the world, we can live lives of peace in the words we speak, in the way we relate to others, in the way we work and love and think. Can there ever be peace unless the world consists someday of peaceful people? We can make sure that we ourselves are the building blocks of peace.*

When my older self looks back at these words I delivered fifty years ago, I do recognize my naivete, speaking to people who perhaps within a few days would be back in the jungle hunting other soldiers with deadly intent and being hunted in return. I may have made life considerably harder for some returning to their missions. Yet I did receive more positive responses to these words than to any of my other messages.

I was also intent on connecting those whom I served to larger Jewish issues. It was one more way to overcome the distance between 'Nam and the "World". On Rosh Hashanah and again on Passover, we mounted a campaign for the United Jewish Appeal as was customary in many congregations back home. The funds we collected, in the hundreds of dollars, were not earth shaking. Yet we wanted to make a statement that our being so far away would not disconnect us from awareness of and responsibility for our people across the globe.

Immediately after Rosh Hashanah, I wrote to my wife:

*It was really wonderful – virtually nothing went wrong, and the smoothness of it really astounded me. There were less men than I thought – between 130-150, but I know that on Yom Kippur we'll probably have more. Some could only come once, and I'm sure they've chosen Yom Kippur.*

*Our quarters were not fancy – regular barracks with rows of double bunks. No such thing as flush toilets here. But it was kind of cool at night and no mosquitos. Actually, living with all the guys was fun, and I enjoyed this aspect. There were a few officers who were kind of upset with the living arrangements. I can understand that because it was so different from what they are used to . . . but I think they got over it.*

*The services went smoothly. Dave Berris, especially, is an excellent cantor – a sweet voice, and he really knows nusach (the liturgical melodies specific to each holiday). Several others helped with parts of the davening. What a pleasure for me. I didn't have to be both rabbi and cantor at once! . . . I blew shofar and read the Torah and, of course, talked and talked and talked. Some seemed to respond to some of my sermons, especially the one on peace which I liked best myself. Our chapel turned out beautifully. Plenty of room, air-conditioned, and we fixed it up nicely as a shul.*

*I tried desperately to make the service one for everyone, and lots of guys did tell me how they appreciated it. For many, it wasn't primarily a religious occasion but a good break from their routines; and I'm glad about that, too. There were a number who called home and used the clubs and other facilities at Cam Ranh. The beach there is phenomenal. I went down twice myself, and you should see the waves; and the sand is beautiful. I'm told that the beaches here are even nicer than in Hawaii.*

*The eating was one of the highlights. The meals all together turned out so beautifully! We had soup, Gefilte fish, TV dinners, honey cake, salad, fruit cocktail and drinks plus matzah and Kiddush! The TV dinners came from Los Angeles and were good – roast beef, meat loaf, chicken, stuffed cabbage plus vegetables and even potato and noodle kugel! Everyone pitched in, and everyone seemed to be happy!*

*For many, more time was spent in Shul than ever before. Some of the guys from the field seemed in paradise. They appreciated many little things like having a bed to sleep in and a snack bar to buy food whenever one is hungry.*

Of course, the unforeseen was bound to happen. Before Rosh Hashanah, the flight from Qui Nhon was delayed for hours, and the group which included Orthodox Jews could not arrive until long after the sun had set. Our services and meal service were complete. Realizing there was nothing that could have been done, these men accepted their plight. We served them a festive meal, and I sat with them long into the evening.

I was soon to face this very problem personally on a trip to An Khe in November. Flights were so frequently delayed or cancelled. I wrote to my wife:

*The flight came in very late – about 5 PM, and then we had to wait a long time to be picked up because of a mistake in information about the flight. As the sun was setting, I was so upset; but I was helpless. So finally, about 7:00 we arrived at the base – long after dark. It was the first time I can remember in about 12 years that I had ridden on Shabbat, but there was nothing I could do so no point in being upset.*

It was rare that I had to fall short of my personal religious commitments, but I knew I was not entirely in control in this war zone.

Before Yom Kippur, the kashrut observant men met to share a meal before the fast. I described our plans to my wife:

*The menu won't be so bad – TV dinners, salad, gefilte fish, and challah! Yes, challah! Mom sent me a package of good things this week including a wonderful small challah she had made. I'll serve it, and everyone will have a little piece, and it will be delicious. As for dessert, you have prepared honey cake!*

My wife, Lorri, and I conspired to surprise everyone by offering a break-the-fast meal after Yom Kippur they would never forget. To do this, we needed generosity and cooperation from special people. Brenner Brothers' Bakery in Seattle was willing to contribute bagels. They would be shipped in sealed bags to preserve their freshness as much as possible. Cream cheese was available locally. We found a way for Lorri to purchase 50 pounds of sliced lox! We knew a navigator from McChord Air Force Base near Tacoma who flew regular supply missions to Vietnam. Airman Brown, who had been active in the Jewish chapel program at adjoining Fort Lewis, was willing to deliver the lox by hand carrying it in his cockpit! Lorri arranged for a Red Cross telegram to reach my desk to notify me of the arrival and location of the lox, an "emergency essential shipment requiring immediate attention" at an airbase in our region. Of course, we sped to pick it up before the tropical sun would render it inedible.

*Breaking the Yom Kippur fast with bagels and lox*

There is no way to describe the looks of amazement on the faces of those men and women as they ended the Yom Kippur fast. Bagels and lox in Vietnam! This was certainly something about which to write home.

I reported to my wife:

*Last night there was almost a packed house – and everyone seemed to be really responsive and together. I chanted Kol Nidre, and Dave Berris did the rest. So many guys helped . . . I feel close to these guys. We even had a few women this time – 2 nurses from An Khe and Qui Nhon, and of course the guys liked that. I met a lot of new men this time. Some had come in from far-off places where they are alone, and I've made a lot of new contacts now which I was hopeful of doing. Today we had services from 9:30-2:30 and then from 4:30-7. Of course, the turnout thinned as the day wore on, but we ended strongly. I was worried about the length and the amount of Hebrew, but we did our best, and the results were encouraging.*

*The white kittel (the white robe worn on Yom Kippur) was passed around to 6 cantors! I actually wore it only once – for Kol Nidre – but since there was only one, the chazan had to have it.*

The High Holidays were memorable, but now reality set in as everyone returned to one's unit. We disassembled our makeshift sanctuary and returned to Nha Trang.

## SUKKOT

Even before the High Holidays, we were planning for the joyful festival of Sukkot. We would be scattered throughout the region, but we hoped to be ambitious. The JWB supplied the four species of the produce of the soil, the lulav and etrog, so vital for this traditional holiday of harvest and thanksgiving. They arrived in excellent condition. Building the sukkah was totally our responsibility. Help at our headquarters in Nha Trang came from a most unusual place.

Our office manager was Sgt. Gunther Haase, a career soldier with a surprising and unexpected history. Born in Germany, he was drafted as a young man into the German Luftwaffe, its Air Force, where he was trained as a pilot. He served during World War II. His plane was shot down by the Allies, and he was captured and imprisoned in a prisoner of war camp. Impressed by the humane treatment he received in captivity, he immigrated after the war to the United States and enlisted in the U.S. Army. In 1970, I imagine that he was in his early to middle fifties. I soon discovered that he was also a master carpenter. When it was time to build our sukkah, he was ready to volunteer. In fact, he was more than ready. He was eager. He quickly took charge, designed the structure, ordered the materials, and, shirtless, set to work. He directed the project ably, enlisting all the chaplains' assistants to help.

This opportunity to offer help especially for the Jewish program was characteristic of Sgt. Haase. I never learned the full story of his journey, but I intuited that he wanted to demonstrate how much he cared for the welfare of our program. In all our many interactions, I never sensed anything but concern and generosity on his part.

I knew then that I would never sit in a sukkah which took form in quite that fashion ever again, designed by a veteran of Germany's armed forces, and built by him along with Catholic, Protestant, and Jewish assistants. Everyone took pride in helping one another. It was one memorable example of interfaith partnership I would witness many times during my tour.

The schach, the covering atop the sukkah, was taken from coconut palm trees which grew in abundance in the area. We decorated with fresh tropical

*Sgt. Haase building the sukkah with Ed Finkelstein*

*Sgt. Haase with Ed Finkelstein and John Kanarek building the sukkah*

fruits and foliage. We even hung carrots and onions to add a note of levity! We were ready to eat our meals and to invite guests to join us in our sukkah.

The design created by Sgt. Haase was easily replicable, and we shared it with all our lay leaders. By the time the holiday arrived, there were four beautiful sukkot constructed at major bases, in Pleiku, Qui Nhon, and Cam Ranh Bay in addition to Nha Trang. Building was not without its challenges. In Pleiku, Charlie Marcus and Chuck Miller scavenging schach in nearby fields came under mortar fire! They emerged unscathed carrying the palm fronds they had found. They were blessed with the fulfillment of the rabbinic dictum: "When one is involved in doing a mitzvah, one cannot be harmed." Sgt. Haase' plans were so useful that they guided the sukkah built in my first position as a synagogue rabbi in Edmonton, Alberta, Canada. I'm not certain that my congregation ever knew that its sukkah was designed by a man who was formerly a German prisoner of war!

On the eve of Sukkot, I was elated at what we had managed to build. I wrote:

*Our Sukkah is gorgeous. You would never believe it possible. It is lush with all kinds of fruit. Tonight, after services, we'll eat there and sing and pretend we are not here and try to imagine we're with those we love.*

I traveled from place to place during the holiday carrying my lulav and etrog. At An Khe, there was no sukkah; but I spent the day thoroughly engaged with the members of our lay led group. I wrote to my wife:

*I arrived here by 11 AM, and have been busy talking with guys, meeting a few new men, visiting some of the old ones, dinner with Dave Berris and then a small get together in the evening. Even the nurse from the hospital came tonight, Marita Silverman. She's from the East Coast, quite Jewish-minded and very unmilitary. It's nice to have a woman in the congregation every so often. We played the Jerusalem tape once again (a video about Jerusalem), and then I took the lulav and etrog out, and most held them and said the words of blessing. They really seemed to appreciate having them brought.*

Sukkot was a whirlwind of activity, and there were moments when we captured the spirit of the holiday. We tried hard to reach people across our vast region. For me, keeping as busy as possible was my strategy for suppressing the sadness of being away from loved ones at a sacred time. I learned how the joy of a holiday can be diminished in direct proportion to the distance one is away from everyone one loves.

## CHANUKAH

On the eve of Chanukah in late December, I was summoned to the office of the Commanding General in our headquarters, Lieutenant General A.S. Collins. It was not every day that I received such an invitation. I had had opportunities to meet the general as we sometimes passed each other in our compound. He was always concerned about my welfare and always asked if I had everything I needed to accomplish my mission.

When I entered his office, he received me warmly and first wanted to know about the wellbeing of the troops I served. What was the state of their morale? I was totally honest when I shared with him that so many were coping but harbored deep reservations about this war. There was no enthusiasm. I told him about Lloyd Kantor and the bitterness he felt in the aftermath of his traumatic injuries. He listened carefully and empathetically. Of course, I understood that he was intent on pursuing his mission despite whatever misgivings he may have held within. I felt that he really understood.

He had called me to his office for a specific reason. He had a dear Jewish friend who had served with him in the same unit many years before. He was Jacob Arvey, a political leader from Illinois who was also active in the Jewish community. He was celebrating his 75th birthday, and it would fall during Chanukah. Could I help General Collins craft an appropriate message? He was eager to include some words in Hebrew in his greeting. I was happy to assist.

Chanukah afforded another opportunity to produce a TV video, so I traveled once more to the studio on the nearby island. I was now more acquainted with possibilities for production. With music in the background, images of the menorah with all its candles aflame and a spinning dreidel dominated. I described the program to my wife:

*We started with a musical background, Maoz Tzur, Rock of Ages, on record. Then Joel (Brauner) and Ed (Finkelstein) did the blessings and lit the candles, and I began my talk. When I mentioned the dreidel, Joel spinned one, and the camera focused close up on it. You should see how beautifully it worked out. At the conclusion, the camera went back to the candles, and the recording of Maoz Tzur played again.*

In my voiceover message, I spoke about how the holiday had evolved from celebrating an unexpected military triumph of the few against the many to an emphasis on a victory of the spirit with the Temple restored. Softer values are at the center. I quoted Zacharia's memorable words which are read during the holiday: "Not by power nor by might but by my Spirit, said the Lord of Hosts."

Chanukah would be a sprint for Ed and me. We created a new dreidel game to play. The four Hebrew letters on the dreidel call to mind the phrase "A great miracle happened there," testifying to the rekindled flame in the Temple in Jerusalem that lasted eight days on a small amount of olive oil as fuel. Our dreidel game was a personal application of the four letters to our present predicament. The "nun" (null) meant that there would be no change in troop levels in Vietnam. The "heh" (halb) predicted that half of the troops would be withdrawn. The most desirable spin would be "gimel" (ganz), a total withdrawal! The worst spin, the "shin" (shtel), augured a surge in troops deployed. We light heartedly put our own spin on politics, but we all had skin in that game! The parties would have candles, singing, the game, movies, gifts, decorations, and latkes. We were off to Pleiku, Phu Cat, Qui Nhon, Cam Ranh Bay, Phan Rang, and, of course, Nha Trang.

Describing our parties in Phi Cat and Qui Nhon on one day, I wrote:

*. . . the singing was good, the movie seemed to go over, even the dreidel game got some laughs, and the food was terrific. Josh was working on latkes all day. I think he even prepared home-made apple sauce. We each had an electric frypan, so we could cook a lot at once. Before we lit candles, I gave a little talk about Russian Jewry, the recent trial, and the relationship of Chanukah and their plight.*

At that moment, show-trials were in progress in the Soviet Union for a group of activists in Leningrad who, oppressed and denied expressions of their Jewishness, conspired to hijack a plane and fly to freedom in Finland. They were apprehended and tried with very harsh penalties pending including execution.

In our monthly bulletin, I had highlighted the plight of Russian Jews:

*Centuries ago, a great Jewish thinker and poet Yehuda Halevi described the Jewish people as mysteriously part of a single body with Israel at its heart. Perhaps he had in mind the uncanny feeling of all Jews for each other regardless of where they are on earth. A time of great triumph or disaster anywhere seems to be shared everywhere almost instantly. This characteristic of Jews has often served our people well especially in times of distress, and today the interdependence of Jews is as crucial as ever before.*

*In recent weeks, the plight of Jews in the Soviet Union has been impressed upon us very strongly. The recent trials have brought to world attention the agony of a people struggling to be able to live as Jews despite a half-century of systematic suppression of everything Jewish life needs to be vibrant. Many Jews especially among the young refused to yield. We hear stories of the young men who for years have eaten no meat because they know that Jews only eat certain kinds, but they know not which, of a young woman who has sewn a cloth of blue and white inside her coat to express her identity, the tears shed by some after receiving secretly a package of prayer books and yarmulkas smuggled to them by a visitor.*

*Our being so far from home does not relieve us of our burdens as Jews. We must respond to this crisis together in any way we can.*

We wanted not only to connect the GIs to critical events around the world but to enable them to be involved. Fred Wenger created a petition which we distributed widely:

## Petition

*We, the undersigned, Jewish chaplains, members of the American Jewish community and concerned men of every faith serving in the Republic of Vietnam are shocked and alarmed at the recent outbreak of show trials and other forms of intimidation launched against the Jews of the Soviet Union. We condemn these trials as a form of public libel levelled against the entire Soviet Jewish community whose members have distinguished themselves in every aspect of Soviet life. We join our voices to those of the worldwide Jewish community in hope that the full weight of international public opinion be marshalled to ensure that justice is done and that more martyrs be not added to the ranks of Israel.*

*We call on the President of the United States, the Soviet ambassador to the United States, and the American ambassador to the United Nations to use their good offices to assure that all accused be given impartial trials open to international inspection, and that all Soviet Jews who wish to emigrate to the State of Israel be at liberty to do so.*

I was inspired by word that my wife had participated in a rally for Soviet Jews in Seattle, one of many across the United States. We wanted Jews in Vietnam to feel bonded to these protests and to fellow Jews in crisis. The response was uniformly excellent, and we gathered many signatures. When news reached us that the sentences first announced were commuted, we rejoiced. We had power which we added to the power of many others.

The party in Cam Ran Bay was the biggest and the best but with one hitch. My previous image of army life included endless scenes of peeling potatoes, but I learned that even potatoes could be in short supply:

*We couldn't find any fresh potatoes, so we had the first Chanukah party ever without latkes! We had some dehydrated mashed potatoes in a can, but, as much as we tried, no latkes. Everyone took the tragic news very well. Instead, we had ice cream, cookies, and soda pop. We showed a new film, too, one which just came from Pioneer Women in New York. It was about immigrants and their readjustment in Beer Sheva. Really well done, and it went over well. Then one of the guys, Ben Stern, who had just come back from a thirty day leave which he had taken in Israel told of some of his impressions, and he did a fine job.*

Our penultimate party was in Nha Trang:

*Chaplain Andrews and Father Wetzel came, our whole office staff, even two Filipino secretaries who work nearby. And about fifteen of our guys, too. For a while, I was worried that we would be outnumbered! But it all worked out beautifully, and everyone seemed to enjoy. We worked hard on the latkes this afternoon, and today we had fresh potatoes, so the party was complete.*

54

That year Christmas fell during Chanukah, and for the first time in my life I attended midnight mass along with Ed at the invitation of Father Wetzel:

*It was a most interesting, elaborate ritual, lots of congregational responses, all in English. The priest gave a short sermon about gift-giving, mutually, and compared it to the exchange between God and man. Sounded a little like our teachings about the covenant. Christmas carols were very beautiful . . . I feel sad for most of the men because I can see that their holidays, too, are perhaps the most difficult of all to face, much less to rejoice.*

Having the opportunity to witness each other's special days was so characteristic in the military. We worked together so closely that it is natural to be included in each other's sacred occasions.

## NEW YEAR 1971

While the New Year is not marked on our sacred calendar, it was especially noted as we marked our time until we would return to the "world". I was surprised to find a visitor from Cam Ranh Bay, Ben Stern, who had just reported on his thirty day leave in Israel where he may return to settle after separating from the Army. Here is how we spent New Year's Eve:

*I had heard about an Israeli who was the proprietor of a hotel and restaurant in Nha Trang. Because the town had been off limits, I never met him before or even tried to find him. In some ways, I expected to find a person who was really an expatriate. Ben and I decided to investigate. We found the hotel, called the Nautique, and it is only a couple of blocks from where I live. Was he glad to see us!! His name is Yeshaia Perez, originally from Casablanca; and he has a family still in Israel. He had worked for years with an international engineering company in a number of countries, but for some reason I don't fully understand had to leave and took over the hotel. And he's doing well. What made me so happy was his greeting and the fact that Israel is very dear to him. In fact, he plans to go back when his present lease is up in April or May. He has interest in Judaism, too, and seems to know something, even offering to serve me fish in new utensils if I want to eat there sometime. We talked in Hebrew most of the time and English, too. He only knows six languages. It was a nice visit, and I invited him over to my office. I hope I can get to see him often. You should see his menu . . . It's just like a good restaurant back home! Of course, the hotel is used for lots of things. We were offered a room and girls several times as we came in and out. Even when the town was off limits, the place is often frequented by GI's and their prostitutes. There were several there last night.*

We did refuse the invitation to spend the night! Despite such distractions, being in the presence of an Israeli and speaking Hebrew were enough to transport us far from the reality of war in Southeast Asia.

Returning late to my room, I spent an uneasy night. Weapons and flares were fired into the air marking the occasion creating a deafening sound. It was scary and unnerving. Somehow I fell into an uneasy sleep.

## TU BISHVAT

No occasion, no matter what its place in the hierarchy of sacred days, is too insignificant for a celebration. In Pleiku, we organized a Tu Bishvat party to celebrate the New Year for trees. I brought a movie about Israel, gave a brief talk, and then we sat down for a meal of salami, French bread, and watermelon which was in season. It was simply delicious. Watermelon in February was a big hit. Even if it is not a fruit harvested from a tree, it served as a welcome symbol of wonder at the abundance of fruit of the earth.

## PURIM

As we had come to expect before every holiday, our office was overcrowded with boxes of hamantaschen and gifts for everyone sent from the JWB and caring volunteers from across the country. It was also nearing the time when my treasured assistant, Ed Finkelstein, would complete his tour and return home. I had grown close to him, and I would sorely miss him.

In February 1971, we convened our second Lay Leaders' conference in Nha Trang to prepare for both Purim and Passover. I described our experience to my wife:

*The services, discussions, meals, and the tour of Nha Trang went so well. The guys got to know each other, and we shared a good many problems and suggestions, . . . Fred Wenger was here, and he really helped a lot at the conference with ideas and comments and about a dozen lay leaders. We had good talks about Purim and Passover plans, and in the afternoon we even had a session on the beach which got us all sunburns. Then a special bus came to take us on a tour of Nha Trang – places I had never been to before. We went through the main market, visited a fish market next to a charming fishing village where all kinds of fresh fish are for sale. And we got a close look at the big Buddha.*

With only one day to celebrate Purim, we knew we would be making a mad dash to bring the reading of the Megillah (the Biblical book of Esther) and a celebration to three congregations, Cam Ranh Bay, Tuy Hoa, and Nha Trang. In Cam Ranh on Purim evening, about twenty guys gathered where we read the Megillah in Hebrew and in English, sang our old favorites for the holiday, distributed gifts, and then sat down together to enjoy hamantaschen, good strong punch, and fellowship. We even collected funds for an orphanage near Tel Aviv, fulfilling the mitzvah of providing gifts for the poor.

Rising at 5 AM on Purim day, I prepared for the journey ahead. I described how the day unfolded to my wife:

*At Tuy Hoa, there was a small group as I had expected, but I had neglected them for Chanukah, so I wanted to be there this time. I arrived by about 9:30, and at 11 we had the service and a beautiful luncheon. And the funniest thing happened. The mess hall provided us with some salads to go with the salami sandwiches. One was potato salad. Well, on top of the salad, made out of fluffy white mashed potatoes, was a cross! I guess my lay leader forgot to tell the mess sergeant that it was a Jewish activity! I noticed that everyone ate around the cross. It returned intact to its source. Only in the Army! We did have a good time. The reading went well, and they enjoyed the groggers and even the kid's songs we sang.*

*I had a chopper coming to pick me up about 2 PM for the flight to Nha Trang which took about an hour. I got back to the chapel, and at 5 PM we had the seudah. I read the Megillah again for them since they hadn't heard it, and then we did have a beautiful seudah. Here's the menu:*

> *French Bread*
> *Salami*
> *Mustard*
> *Kugel (my best!)*
> *Assorted Vegetables*
> *Gefilte Fish*
> *Horseradish*
> *Champagne & Wine*
> *Hamantaschen*
> *Watermelon*

*Yes, I know some of the things just don't go together! Well, here I've found any Jewish foods can be mixed, and they please.*

*After that marathon, Norm Kass and I debated the relative merits of the Latke and Hamantasch – the theme being "The Shape of World Peace"!! We argued whether the circular latke or the triangular hamantasch symbolized the most favorable pathway to peace in the world. He was really good. What a wit he has! And the guys liked that.*

*Then I presented a plaque to Ed (Finkelstein) from the II Corps Jewish Community and gave a little speech about him. He too gave a little speech, and I think he really liked the plaque.*

After reading the Megillah three times at three locations, I was thoroughly exhausted. It was especially hard to say goodbye to Ed who had gone way beyond the call of duty to make our program successful. There was no detail too small or humble to which he would not devote himself. Relationships in Vietnam formed quickly and deeply, and then one had to learn to let go as the men would move to other units or to return home. Ed would go on to successful positions of leadership in the Jewish community as Executive Director of Jewish Community Centers.

It would be a while before a new assistant would arrive, so I braced myself for the period of being shorthanded. I knew that others in my office would help fill the gap.

## PASSOVER

The weeks before the holiday were occupied with communications and detailed arrangements for everyone to assemble in Nha Trang. We planned for a large crowd, knowing that some would be unable to come due to their duties.

I urged everyone to come in our monthly bulletin:

*Passover is certainly the most popular of our special days, a time when in an atmosphere of leisure and feasting and surrounded by our loved ones we renew our ties to our heritage. Of course, a basic ingredient is missing this year for each of us, but I promise that we will do our best to fill the void by making the days together as much like home as possible.*

*Please be sure to mark off on your calendars Friday, 9 April to Monday, 12 April. We hope to bring everyone to Nha Trang which by unanimous acclaim is THE place to be in Military Region 2. Our seders will be complete from knaidlach to charoset. Of course, we will have services and a few special surprises, but also you will have a good chance to make some new friendships, perhaps restore a few old ones, and to refresh yourself with some of those golden rays on our beautiful beach. Incidentally, as I write this, the sunlight is flowing brightly through my window; so, I predict super weather for our celebration. Your lay leader will soon have for you copies of the MACV letter which authorizes you to come. Be sure to be in touch with him because he will coordinate travel arrangements and answer any questions you may have.*

The kosher for Passover food was due to arrive a few short days before the holiday. I admit my anxiety as we awaited the deliveries. I had already learned that there was a tremendous amount of theft and dealing in foodstuffs throughout Vietnam. My worst nightmare was to face the seders without dinners to serve! At a moment of relief, I wrote home:

*All the food is in! I saw it today, and it's amazing. Frozen dinners, gefilte fish, chicken soup, horseradish, macaroons, peaches, even kosher cokes! I am so relieved it is all here. We should have ample food. And you'll never guess. Two cases of walnuts! The herring hasn't come yet – but maybe in the next two days.*

Cooperation among all our partners to prepare for the holiday was exceptional. The housing, chapel, snacks, mess hall, trips into town for recreation were all falling into place. As usual, I was finding great people to lend us a hand.

While it is not unusual back home to find model seders especially for children in Jewish schools, I did not expect that a model seder would take place here in a war zone. Yet my Christian colleagues were insistent, so I led a seder just for them. The degree of sharing and curiosity about each other was a source of much satisfaction for me.

It was customary to invite the generals in our compound to our seder. One memorable response was received. I recalled the event:

*One of the generals called to ask if we could change the date of the seder! It seems that several congressmen will be here then. This morning, General Brown, the commanding general, came into my office to assure me that he hadn't made such a request and explained that he wouldn't come because of the visit and offered his regrets. He is a nice fellow, brash but very competent and respected, but we all got a good laugh over the other general's request. Some experiences in the Army I will never forget.*

While the brass were otherwise occupied, we were joined at the seder table by fellow chaplains, their assistants, and students and faculty from the local Protestant Seminary. We even had Buddhist priests experiencing Passover for the first time. It was an interfaith event.

In preparation for the seders, I had kashered a large vat in which the charoset would be made. The young Vietnamese women who were helping us were adorable. Wearing brightly colored kippot that we had supplied and having rolled up their sleeves, they stood on chairs to be able to reach deeply into the vat to mix by hand the chopped walnuts, raisins, other chopped fruits, and wine. They laughed heartily and chatted happily as they prepared this strange dish for our seder.

I wrote this message to the arriving troops:

*Early in the seder service, we read: "Kol dich-feen yay-tay v'yay-chul. Kol ditz-reech yay-tay v'yif-sach." "All who suffer, come eat with us, all who are in need come celebrate the Passover with us." Probably no one among us comes really hungry, although there are, no doubt, certain kinds of food you crave. From knaidlach to charoset, our seders will be complete. In a deeper sense though, this is a year in which all of us learned something of suffering, and each of us is in need. The seder with all its familiar practices, its symbols, its songs, its festive atmosphere, has something important to give each of us. And I truly hope that you will go back with a little more strength because of our fellowship.*

Separate barracks were set aside for the arrivals. We were excited as we welcomed at least 100 soldiers. I was somewhat disappointed at first by the lower-than-expected turnout, but they were a happy and appreciative crowd. After the first two days with their seders had passed, I reflected:

*I think everyone who came had a good time. Our seders went so well. The food we had was so abundant that we have loads and loads left over. So much that we've been giving the guys as much as they can carry to take home . . . Our services turned out well, too, lots of participation and attendance was good. Today we were a little hurried because of the Easter service at 11. We had an appeal, too, and collected about $300, I think, which I thought was quite good. It will go to the United Jewish Appeal.*

*Best of all has been the feeling of the guys. They all seemed to fit together, and a lot of friendships were formed. Most I already knew, but there were a few, especially from far-out places and a few new arrivals, whom I met for the first time. Really, all in all, it was as good as I could have hoped. The weather was perfect, and the tours of Nha Trang we arranged, and the beach were thoroughly enjoyed. I went today to the beach with them – about a mile walk –, and it was so gorgeous. I have a good sunburn.*

After the first seder, we decided to send some of our kosher meals to Yeshia Perez at the Nautique as a gesture of friendship. We had invited him to join our seder, but he was unable to accept. I asked for a few volunteers to be our emissaries, and the response was overwhelming. I think that the reputation of his "hotel" had made the rounds. We dispatched the meals, and I could only hope that the men would resist the urge to spend the night!

With the first two days of the holiday past, it was quiet in Nha Trang. We dismantled our temporary "shul" and returned all our supplies to their proper places. When the last two days of Passover arrived, I knew not to expect a crowd. A small group gathered for morning prayers, and I gathered up my courage to prepare matzah brei to add to the Kiddush. While I was a novice cook, I followed my wife's careful step by step recipe. The result was well received!

Very soon after Passover, I had a wonderful reunion with my wife in Hawaii. Returning with anticipated sadness upon still another separation, I spent a Shabbat in Cam Ranh Bay:

*Being in Cam Ranh was probably the best possible therapy. Lots of guys (16 last night), good conversation, friends really helped an ailing rabbi with a heartsick separation syndrome. I always get such a good welcome here and am made to feel so much at home. The guys are still talking about Passover and Nha Trang, and they have so much food which was left over. Everyone is eating gefilte fish in Cam Ranh! "Jewish soul food" is how it's known.*

There were few times when my religious requirements interfered with my duties, but one humorous incident occurred as the days of counting the Omer connecting Passover to Shavuot unfolded. Plans were being made to observe Memorial Day in our compound. I was invited to take part, but I was not shaving during this period in accordance with tradition. This is a period of semi-mourning. I consulted with Chaplain (Col) Andrews, and we concluded that it would be best for me not to take a public role before the commanding officers when my facial hair would at that moment be hard to miss. They would have no idea why I was growing a beard. It would be best for me to keep a lower profile!

## SHAVUOT

With the number of troops declining rapidly and Shavuot having less cachet than other major festivals, our program would be small and lonely. Shavuot comes at the conclusion of a careful counting of days of the Omer. Every one of us serving in Vietnam was familiar with mindful counting of days. I wrote in our monthly bulletin:

*Up to Shavuot, we count the Omer, our own yearly countdown from the exodus to a more profound kind of freedom, the revelation at Sinai. I hope that you are proceeding well with your own special countdowns.*

With fewer Jews around and fewer still able to attend, our services were small. It was the most difficult of sacred days as I expected. Yet the absence of spirit and numbers was eased by the approach of the end of my tour.

# One on One

*With Steve Shapiro*

While sacred occasions in the calendar served as oases from the dangers of war and from the burden of being so far from home, one on one encounters which occurred every day proved to be crucial. I saw my mission virtually each day to reach out to make contact and to be a listening ear. There were more than a few days when I would travel for hours across our region to find one or two fellow Jews who were posted in isolated, far-off encampments. There were also times when I spent a day searching for Jews and came up empty. I reported on my first helicopter ride to my wife:

*I was a little scared, but I was with four priests and one Protestant chaplain, so I had to feel safe. We went to several firebases – bases for a large unit from which smaller units go out to patrol the area . . . I carried along my big chaplain's kit complete with a little Ark, Torah, and books, and stocked with wine and Hebrew national cans as treats. But – after all that – on all the stops, I couldn't find even one Jew.*

That experience was the exception. I was determined to locate the men I was serving.

I was happiest when spending quality time with individuals. Uniformly, I found that my visits, often showing up unannounced at an office or other place of duty, were welcomed. Even in first time meetings, getting to the heart of the matter did not take much time. I found that the overwhelming majority were opposed to the war and were stricken with the knowledge that they were contributing to the war effort. There were exceptions, especially among career soldiers who believed in the mission. They were very few.

It was clear to me that the widespread protests back home took a palpable toll on the spirit of these GI's. Adding to the constant pangs of conscience and their own sense of powerlessness was the often meaningless and boring work they were called upon to do in their units. I deeply empathized. I thought listening to be a meager offering, but it did seem to bring some relief. It was safe to talk to a chaplain.

So many men in this uncomfortable situation seemed to adjust to their unhappy state, knowing that their year would elapse; and they could be finished with this war simply by biding their time. There was no enthusiasm.

While my mission was directed to Jewish personnel, my travels often gave me opportunities to meet others. I clearly recall one day when I was ferried by helicopter to a barren firebase atop a hill, and I learned quickly that there were no Jews stationed there. Instead, the commander, a Lt. Colonel, showed me around his position. We spoke, and it soon was apparent that he carried his own questions about the war. Yet, this was his third tour. He shared with me that he had sought this mission because he felt that he was skilled in protecting the lives of the men under his command. Saving lives was his goal. I strongly felt that he, too, disliked this war.

I wrote home about another encounter:

*I met with two black men this morning who are C.O.s (Conscientious Objectors) and medics. They wanted to make sure that they wouldn't be put in a combat situation. One was a minister's son and Seventh Day Adventist, the other Pentecostal. Both are deeply religious – gentle and honest guys. I enjoyed meeting with them immensely. I was able to give them the reassurances that they sought. It's so good to be able to do things for these men.*

I did meet several men who approached me for help with their applications for conscientious objector status while in uniform and in a war zone. Such steps were a longshot at best. I could and did write letters on their behalf testifying to the sincerity of their claims, but I do not know if their efforts were successful. Once in Vietnam, changing one's status was unlikely.

I counseled one man in An Khe who was deeply troubled. I wrote:

*One guy who I feel attached to is an infantryman and wants to apply as a C.O. He has had to go out into the field, but he never has loaded his gun and cannot conceive of shooting at anyone. He is really receiving a lot of harassment from officers and NCOs. I'm going to try to help him.*

Another, a medic, also did not want to go out on patrol in the future. It took much courage to buck the system in this way. Their fates were still undecided.

I do recall meeting one Jewish medic who was a C.O. serving his time in uniform as a noncombatant. He was assured that he would not be attached to a combat unit, but on arrival he found that he was assigned to support such a unit. He appealed, and he asked for a letter from me. I wrote the letter, and I was heartened that his request was honored. He was placed in another unit.

Counseling those who suffered from the ravages of war was frequent. In Song Mao, I spent time with a soldier who was a crew member in a tank. It was struck by a rocket, and the two soldiers riding next to him were killed instantly. He was thrown from the tank and was unconscious, but he was only lightly injured. He spoke calmly of the incident, but I knew that the trauma was deep and would be lasting.

I grew close to Charlie, a green beret whom I had first met at Fort Lewis. He was assigned to a team of twelve GIs who worked with a unit of 300 Montagnard tribesmen on the Cambodian border. I described him to my wife:

*He is a very bright and sensitive guy, really searching as a Jew. At Fort Lewis, I gave him a few of Heschel's books, and one was blown apart in his backpack during a mortar attack on his post. He was just slightly injured. He so much longs to go home to seclude himself and study Jewish tradition. I loaded him up with kosher food, candles, wine, books, and a tallit; and we're going to send him things regularly. He loves to talk theology and is concerned about his relationship with God. He is also very disturbed by what we are doing here . . . It was good to meet a man who is trying to face the moral issue. I feel that very few are deeply bothered. Mostly they try to get by, to surmount much smaller personal problems – loneliness and boredom. Charlie came here feeling he could do some good.*

As time passed, after repeated visits, I saw how his experience of the war and many firefights were taking their toll. He had killed people, and he was suffering. On one occasion, he came to my office to give me a survival belt which he insisted that I wear always in my travels. It included a knife, a firearm, water purification pills, and even a pill I could use to kill myself in an extreme situation. I tried respectfully to accept his gift without the weapons. He finally understood.

On another occasion while we were standing one evening in a lighted area on the grounds of my compound, he pushed me gruffly away from the light. I was unnecessarily exposing myself to potential danger by standing in the light! He was perpetually on edge.

Finally, he had had enough. He came to me in desperation seeking a reassignment to a non-combatant's role. He was interested in becoming a chaplain's assistant. By pulling some strings, we were able to have him placed in Saigon aiding the rabbi in his work.

I was not spared the violence of the war with its awful toll. Within a few weeks of my arrival, I was called in to officiate at the memorial service for an airman. I wrote:

*I received a call from Phan Rang Air Force Base from my lay leader. There had been a rocket, one rocket, about an hour before which hit the base. One fatality – one of our guys. I don't even know who it is yet, but tomorrow I will go there to try to conduct a memorial service for him . . . How terrible I feel, really sick to my stomach. Life is so fragile and cheap here. I feel terribly for his family back home. Somehow I am going to write a eulogy for him. I knew this would have to happen here. I feel so inadequate – almost without any words.*

His name was Richard Pearl. We had not met. I wrote:

*The story is so tragic. The man was married, about 32, very well-liked by everyone. I came here this afternoon and talked to his commander and to several of his friends. He was genuinely a good man. The part which makes the event especially tragic was that he was due to leave for home this Friday and was on his way to begin out-processing when the rocket came. I never met him, but I found it easy to talk about him. His commander gave a tribute, and our lay leader did a reading. We had a tape made of the service which we will send to his wife. Afterwards, I got together with many of our guys, and there was such a feeling of closeness between us.*

It was the first time in my rabbinic life that I was asked to eulogize a person I had not known. I spoke in the chapel at Phan Rang:

*There is something terribly shattering about our tragedy . . . When a man is taken from our midst as was Richard, it's as if a fruit which has just ripened, full of potential to give, has been destroyed. Richard carried so many hopes of all who knew him and loved him. Perhaps one of the deepest tragedies of this war, of all wars, is that our best young people, just on the eve of expressing their uniqueness, of remaking and reforming the world about them, are cut off. Their hush is so agonizing. What might have been tortures our souls.*

*Your presence tonight is a great testimony to Richard. He was known by everyone, and everyone who knew him thought highly of him. Both his superiors and his peers alike respected and loved this man for his energy, his dedication, his concern for all those around him. He was a man who stood out for his excellence, who took pride in a job well done. He was a friend who was genuine. We are all diminished by his loss . . .*

*To explain his passing is unimaginable. All we are left with is a mandate, a command. We must use fully the miracle of memory to cause Richard to live on in our own lives, to make his friendship, his example, a motivating force for each of us . . . There is something very real about our ability, the power of each of us present, to give an extension of life to one who is gone by the way we remember, by the way we live. May we resolve determinedly to give life to Richard's memory.*

*All who have felt this tragedy know well that in war there can be no winner. Let us pray that mankind will in our day realize the outrage of war, that all will find a way to peace. May Isaiah's words finally be taken from the page where they have lain too long and be fashioned into a world of peace.*

*Nation shall not lift up sword against nation. Nor shall they learn war anymore.*

It would not be long before I would witness the carnage of war on the body and spirit of someone I had come to know and to love. I pick up the narrative from the beginning of my memoir. Lloyd Kantor lay in his bed at the 91st Evacuation Hospital in Chu Lai with the stumps of his four limbs bandaged and bound, the consequence of igniting an explosive booby trap while on patrol. It was the most horrific scene I had ever witnessed. Here was this terribly stricken young man who had been the embodiment of youthful energy and optimism. For three days and nights, I tried to be a support for him, watching as he alternated between anger and hopelessness. When a general visited to pin a Purple Heart on his hospital gown, he struggled mightily to restrain the anger he felt. After stabilizing against great odds, Lloyd was taken to a waiting helicopter that would be his first step on the way to a hospital in Japan. I wrote:

*He is a miracle. He has simply inspired everyone who has seen him by his will. He can even smile and joke, and I just know he will make it. His mother sent a message to him which really cheered him up, and she should be able to see him in Japan...I feel today that were it just to be with this one man during this whole year, I did have a mission here. I've never felt so needed in all my life. I've never felt the tragedy of this war so sharply as I have when he was lying before me. It is just awful.*

In the weeks and months that followed, my wife and I found ways to keep abreast of Lloyd's progress as he went from Japan to Walter Reed Medical Center in Washington, DC, to rehabilitation in the Veterans' Administration hospitals. We were in touch with his mother and his girlfriend Loretta, who stood by him in every excruciating step. Lloyd and Loretta would marry less than a year later. My wife visited him, and she was deeply taken with him. I wrote to her:

*I'm so glad you went to be with Lloyd. He has the potential for greatness. If greatness can be measured by how a man responds to his condition, he has achieved greatness already. We won't ever forget him no matter where we are.*

Amidst the uncounted traumas of this war, the incident which involved Lloyd attracted special attention. A report was aired within a day or two on Walter Kronkite's evening news on CBS, and Lloyd himself was interviewed along with other wounded veterans years later on 60 Minutes.

As the trauma with Lloyd was unfolding, there was a secondary personal drama that stirred within me. At the end of the week, I was scheduled to fly from Saigon to Honolulu for an R & R reunion with my newlywed wife. For me as for so many others, those dates were sacred. We longed to be together.

My quandary was that I knew I could not leave Lloyd's bedside while he fought for his life. Outside, long dark nights and monsoon rains persisted. I feared I would have to tell my wife that our reunion would be delayed. It felt miraculous that Lloyd stabilized sufficiently to be airlifted to Japan while the weather cleared just in time for me to make my flight to Hawaii. For the remainder of my life, I knew that I would never experience such a journey from the most agonizing of moments to the joy of reunion, from darkness to light.

While I waited at the airport in Nha Trang for my flight to Saigon and then on to Hawaii, I tried to process what had transpired in a letter to my wife:

*There were many moments this week when I didn't think this moment would come. The heavy rains and the report of a new typhoon coming, the long days and nights with Lloyd where I didn't know if he would live or die, and he seemed to need me there with him…But the rains passed, and the weather is crystal clear and blue skies now, and Lloyd is doing well in Japan. Now I know we are going to be together, and I'm sure, too, that it will be like heaven.*

Beyond the outer wounds that war mercilessly inflicts, there were other less visible but terribly painful personal issues and crises that arose. Marriage was sorely tested by deployment so far from home. I recall one sergeant who came to me with marital problems. He asked that I write on his behalf asking for compassionate leave so that he could be with his wife. Fortunately leave was granted, and he returned feeling that their relationship had improved. Another man returned from R & R with his engaged wife to be. Soon thereafter the engagement was broken. The stress of separation proved to be too much to bear.

At times, the sanctity of marriage was vulnerable due to separation. One soldier reported to me that his wife had become pregnant from another man, and she wanted a divorce. Hearing this news from thousands of miles away made him so sad and angry. He needed to return home to face the reality of his disintegrating marriage. He was granted compassionate leave; and, on his return, he concluded that divorce was the best solution. Witnessing his grief, I tried to comfort him. I wrote to my wife:

*He even has one child. I don't know how a man can face a situation like that. These casualties of war are not even counted, but I think they're as devastating as any physical hurt can be.*

At least we were able to assure that he could travel immediately to make crucial decisions that were needed.

A young doctor in Cam Ranh Bay returned home twice to be with his wife who suffered bouts of depression largely due to their separation. After his second emergency leave, he did not have to return to Vietnam. The effects of the war marked the lives not only of the soldiers but their dear ones, too. There is a wide circle of loved ones encircling every GI. The impact on one ripples out to others.

While it was unusual to be able to lend a helping hand with quick results, occasionally it happened. A young airman had experienced marital problems with his young wife who was also in the Air Force back home. Their issue was difficulty in communication. On the spot, we decided to place a phone call directly to his wife. I had known the couple who were active in my military congregation at Fort Lewis. I reached her, and we spoke about the problems they faced. She seemed eager to do what was necessary to work on their marriage. Then, handing the phone to the husband, I listened as they resolved to do better and to apologize for misunderstandings. It was surely a special day for this young airman, his wife, and for me as a mediator.

One day, a young GI came to my office in distress. He had recently returned from spending his R & R with a young woman to whom he was engaged. After a short period had elapsed, he learned that she was pregnant. He was upset because he and she had not intended to marry for at least two years. He was in love with his girlfriend, but the timing was not right. After counseling, he concluded that he would meet his responsibility and push up his marriage date.

Conversion and marriage, frequent themes back home, entered even in Vietnam. A non-Jewish soldier who was seeing a Jewish woman was determined to pursue a path to conversion. I was impressed with his seriousness of purpose and described him to my wife:

*There is one guy here whom I had known but hadn't seen for some time. He isn't Jewish yet, but has been searching, and you have no idea how excited he is about Judaism. He reads and thinks a lot and works himself into a state of real excitement. He recently has been going with a Jewish woman. This afternoon we got together, and he was telling me about her and how their relationship developed. I almost began to cry because so much of what he said seemed to describe our relationship. He talked about sharing, about feeling he could be complete, could do so much more because of and through her.*

While full engagement in a program leading to conversion was all but impossible, this man wanted to learn and came asking for recommendations for further study. We welcomed him to join in our ongoing classes in Can Rahn Bay.

One day a civilian contractor who was Jewish asked to see me. He was married to a Vietnamese woman. She was interested in learning more about Judaism, and we were his resource. Having rabbis sent to Vietnam by the military served a need for other Jews whose life path had brought them to this country. I did all that I could to provide materials for learning for this couple.

There were many other varieties of stress aside from marriage. One man insisted on growing a beard which he felt was a mandate of Jewish law. In the modern armed forces, that choice would not be problematic. Fifty years ago, facial hair was prohibited. I was able to speak to his commander, and I hoped that he would be left alone.

More serious and consequential was a young man who faced a court martial for insubordination, disobeying orders, and petty larceny. I described his situation to my wife:

*It is serious because all the charges together could result in a long jail term. Tomorrow I'm going to meet with his defense attorney to see if I can help. He is not a criminal and I think is being permanently hurt by the harassment and the threat of confinement. For over a month he has been kept with some others who are charged in a tent where he must stay. He didn't even have basic needs like a toothbrush and toothpaste.*

I was asked by his defense attorney to appear at the trial as a witness on his behalf. I described the prospect of testifying to my wife:

*Remember the fellow to whose trial I was supposed to go? It was postponed. His defense counsel meanwhile left, and a new one was appointed. Just by chance, I know the new guy from Fort Lewis! We used to meet in the stockade often. The prosecutor is a member of our congregation here in An Khe, and I am certain that he would rather not prosecute this case. I had a meeting with the defendant who is in so much trouble, then with his lawyer, and then both together. I'm more hopeful now. If it goes to trial, I'll probably be coming up in about two weeks to be a mitigation and extenuation witness. But there's a chance that in lieu of court-martial, he may just be discharged which we all agree would be the best thing for him. It's such a sad case. His father committed suicide just before he entered military service, and I know that he has not come to terms with that great loss. The Army experience has really been bitter for this man. I hope it's not going to be complicated more by confinement.*

I was overjoyed when the trial was cancelled, and the defendant was simply discharged from service!

At times, the issue was straightforward, and it was easy to intervene. A religious doctor was scheduled to return home a few days after Yom Kippur.

I supported his petition for a drop of several days to enable him to spend the most sacred day in the Jewish calendar with his wife and family. The request was immediately granted.

A common source of distress was assignment to the war zone where one's special skills were never used. One doctor in Ban Me Thuot was thoroughly distressed for this reason. I wrote:

*The doctor, an internist from Cincinnati, is terribly depressed having almost nothing to do which uses his training. There seems to be an awful lot of men in this situation, especially physicians. Imagine being so far from home and having virtually nothing to do on top of it.*

I met other doctors in Cam Ranh Bay who felt that they had little to do. That sense of needless waste was so commonly expressed. I was powerless to change this reality, but I could at least empathize. The prospect of spending a year of one's life facing emptiness without being able to contribute meaningfully weighed heavily. I could offer salamis and gefilte fish which would bring a fleeting smile and comfort. Mostly I could bring a listening ear.

In my headquarters, I came to know a physician who had already invested 17 years in the Army. He was soon to be promoted to full colonel. I wrote:

*He is really unhappy – feels that in his last several years he has lost so much as a doctor because of the posts he has had. Now, he is the staff surgeon in the same headquarters with me and has almost nothing to do. He will be out after three more years; but, as a doctor, he thinks these years have been a terrible waste. What a tragedy to have to admit that.*

Wasting valuable time and a sense of directionless were common themes. I worked closely with one man who seemed to always carry within him an uncommon anger and resentment. When he returned home, I learned that he often couldn't sleep and had contemplated suicide. It was suspected that he had turned to drugs for relief. His family and friends were terribly worried as they reached out to him to offer support.

Another sensitive GI was able to articulate his struggle:

*He seems to feel much guilt about this year – its wastefulness, the parts of himself that it has brought out and which he abhors. Yet he feels that if he had to do it again, he'd probably be carried along the same path. I appreciate his problem – almost powerlessness about his own self and destiny. There is lots of guilt among the men. Many rationalize but don't articulate it as well as he. But it is there nonetheless. "So why Yom Kippur?" he asks, if we are so powerless over our own destinies?*

The toll taken by participation in the war is hard to underestimate. The nation was committed to a war that was so morally questionable. The draft called virtually every young man to serve. Most did not choose to resist. Yet they carried their doubts with them to Vietnam where they festered. It felt as though they were carried along unwillingly. They felt powerless, and they felt that a valuable part of their youthful energy and dreams was sacrificed on that wasteful altar.

A source of anguish to me was the fleeting quality of the contacts I had with the people I served. Especially when painful issues were raised by an individual, I found that distance and movement made it exceedingly difficult to follow up and to maintain contact. I often could not find out the disposition of a particular problem. On occasion, there was an exception. I wrote:

*I had one experience that made me happy. I went to have my smallpox vaccination when a sergeant came up to me. He had been to my office about two months ago regarding marital problems, and I had written a letter for him recommending that he be granted a compassionate leave which came through. It seems that he did go home, and all is now much improved. He just couldn't thank me enough although what I did was truly little.*

I did long for more continuity which would allow deeper friendship and more trust. My life on the move over such a wide area and the constant movement of troops made sustained encounters virtually impossible.

One factor that influenced my work and my contact was the overall drawdown of troops during my tour. I wrote home:

*. . . it is a reality: 150,000 by next May. It seems that hopefully by the time I come home, all our combat troops will be gone, too. In my travels, I can see the preparations being made. Several places I visit regularly now, Tuy Hoa, Song Mao, even An Khe are rumored to be closing down. Probably all year, I'll be having fewer men and fewer places to visit. What a blessing! For once I think I will rejoice if I have less to do because the men are going home.*

As men that I came to know and love prepared to return home, we were in a position to help ease their reentry into the United States. My wife was living in Seattle not far from Fort Lewis where out-processing took place for many. She and her family were eager to invite the new arrivals over for a home-cooked meal. It was an opportunity to share their joy and to hear first-hand how I was faring. At times, for a single man returning home, the welcome included a date with a local eligible woman!

# 8 Sex, Drugs, and Race

Eye opening for me was the pervasive culture of sex and drugs among the GIs about which we had been warned. Whatever naivete I carried was swiftly swept away. There was no way to miss the very public evidence. Perhaps this is true of every war; but the special burdens of this war, I think, exacerbated these issues as soldiers sought relief and comfort.

On my first visit to the Nautique to spend time with my new Israeli friend, Yeshai Perez, I recall my shock at having to navigate a phalanx of young women as I departed. I was thoroughly groped as I determinedly walked away. There was no subtlety in these women's quest for customers.

One night as I walked from my office to my quarters along a dark street, I was aware of being followed by a woman. She came closer and closer; and, as I reached the entrance to my compound, she came up to me. With her words which I could not understand, and her hands trying to embrace and touch me, she was emphatically trying to be hired for the evening. It took some effort to free myself gently and to refuse.

Prostitution was big business. One day after dinner with a group of local chaplains, we went for a ride in two jeeps and passed by one of the Army compounds with large barracks for enlisted men. We slowed down as we noticed the shocking scene before us. Just outside the perimeter of the camp, there was a long line of motorcycles. Sitting atop or beside them were many young men and young women. Apparently, the men were husbands or brothers accompanying the women. They awaited a steady stream of GIs emerging from the camp who would come out to choose among the women and then take them back to their barracks. I was in disbelief seeing how public these transactions were. Clearly the command looked away and did not interfere. The scene was a graphic picture of how our military presence corrupted both the GI's and Vietnamese families in which young men would willingly offer wives and sisters in return for monetary gain.

It is possible that the Army quietly did some health checks to prevent sexually transmitted diseases. I am not certain. I do know that STDs were rampant. One physician at Qui Nhon told me of one report that there were 1250 cases of STDs for every 1000 troops! Many men were repeatedly treated for disease. Clearly the problem was epidemic.

I have described my visits to Song Mao where small units were stationed. The facilities were basic with no amenities enjoyed at larger bases. The men were isolated with little to do when they were not on duty. After my first visit here, I described what I had seen to my wife:

*It is terribly poor – the housing, clothing, sanitation is about as primitive as you can imagine. Roads aren't paved, litter everywhere, kids running around naked, people with seemingly nothing to do. Of course, the women – if they are young – can be prostitutes. It's incredible how many whores the war has produced and how much the men use them. I've even heard of a few men who love this place and volunteer to come back because of the women here and their availability. I often wonder what the Vietnamese men must think of GIs and the U.S. when we have done so much damage to the women.*

I was aware that many men chose Hong Kong or Bangkok as R & R destinations because of the ready availability of prostitutes. One young lieutenant argued that the Army should sponsor brothels in Vietnam because otherwise there would be few ways to guard against disease. Men would seek out prostitutes one way or another. To try to argue for abstinence or the sanctity of sex would be a losing battle.

The ready supply of potent drugs presented still another huge challenge which could be more deadly. I was called to a special meeting in Qui Nhon for chaplains on the crisis. I wrote:

*The conference is a special one on drugs, probably the worst problem*

79

*among the men right now. It is so widespread, the drugs are so cheap, and the troops are so vulnerable, a combination perfect to encourage drug use. The morning centered around an interview with an addict who was open and honest about himself. Heroin seems to be the problem. About 10-30% of enlisted men seem to be at least experimenting. It is frightening. On the whole, the presentation helped me understand the causes better and to give a little direction in working with the men.*

*I haven't seen too many guys myself who are really in trouble, but the Jewish guys seem to be more the exception. Just on Monday, one fellow did come in and told me of his experiences with cocaine. Fortunately, he has seemed to overcome the problem.*

I reported to my wife about another high-level conference:

*I went to a Drug Suppression Council meeting with a lot of bigwigs – colonels. There is a tremendous amount of concern and awareness of the problem. Much material is being distributed to help educate about the dangers. One of the most promising developments is an "Amnesty Program" whereby guys on drugs can turn themselves in for treatment without fear of criminal proceedings against them. Trouble is, it's not long-term rehabilitation which so many need, but it is in a good direction.*

Marijuana and heroin were cheap and potent. I recall hearing in Nha Trang alone that eighteen troops were admitted to the hospital for heroin overdoses in one day. I could see the disposed paraphernalia of drug use cast on the ground even in the compound of our headquarters.

I was approached by the commander of a military police unit for help in programming against drug use. The Army did offer training programs to warn about both drug use and sexual adventures. There were regular "character guidance" classes in which I and other chaplains participated. The subject often was the danger incurred when soliciting for sex or purchasing drugs. Their impact seemed to be minimal.

Racism raised its ugly head as well. I wrote:

*In Nha Trang last week just after a U.S.O. show, there was a full – scale riot; and there have been a rash of smaller incidents. Between that and drugs, the Army is beset by problems – big problems. My feeling is that Vietnam is a big factor in precipitating them. I doubt if we will ever admit the amount of harm we are doing to our own men by remaining here. It is so maddening.*

Racism was an issue in the military although it rarely surfaced in the Jewish program. African American soldiers were represented in the Army by far more than their percentage in the population. They enlisted in greater numbers, and they were drafted more frequently without as much resistance and without as many deferments as white draftees. I was impressed when at a chaplains' conference in Nha Trang:

*A chaplain came from Saigon to show a film and talk about a new program in race relations. He is an unusual guy, a sociologist, writer, studied at Yale and the U. of Chicago, taught at several universities – was involved in confrontation with Gov. Faubus in Arkansas and now is doing some creative things in the Army.*

My impression in my travels was that the military was more attentive to problems of race and more progressive than U.S. society more broadly.

# 9 Interfaith Relationships

*With Rabbi Lewis at top left, chaplains welcome the Chief of Chaplains*

One of the brightest lights in the military chaplaincy is the way that faith leaders treat one another. During the period that I served, chaplains were Christian or Jewish. Today's armed forces are inclusive of Muslims and other faiths and their religious needs as well.

An apt symbol of mutual respect and cooperation is the typical chapel which we used for religious services and gatherings. While most soldiers committed to a faith were Christian, the small minority of Jews were treated totally as equals. The furnishing of the chapel was completely non-denominational. No religious symbols were permanently displayed. Instead, the sanctuary could be easily welcoming to every religious group. At times, alternate arrangements for the pulpit with appropriate symbols could simply be rolled out on wheels from the wall at the front of the pulpit in which they were stored.

Priests, pastors, and rabbis trained together in the Army's Chaplain's School at Fort Hamilton in New York and spent a basic fitness training stint at Fort Dix in New Jersey. We lived together, and we learned more intimately about beliefs and practices of each other.

That high bar for partnership was manifest wherever we were posted. My office was adjacent to the senior Protestant and Catholic chaplains in my region. While they far outranked me (colonel and lieutenant colonel to captain), there was never a sense of hierarchy. I was treated as an equal in every way. There was nothing they would not do to help me be successful in my mission. I was constantly asked if there was any support I needed. I was invited to fully share in the duties of the office. At times, I represented the chaplains at the daily briefing with key commanders. The office staff never said no when extra help was needed to set up for a program, to build our sukkah, to arrange for my flights, to print materials, and to help move supplies for the Jewish program which at times overwhelmed our office space. The staff chaplain, Joe Andrews, treated me like a son from the day I arrived. At the very end he was generous in evaluating my work and tried in every way possible to seek a drop for me so that I could arrive home a few days earlier than scheduled.

On the National Day of Prayer and on Memorial Day when we convened programs for everyone in our compound, I or lay members of my program were consistently given a major role. When special guests visited including the Army's Chief of Chaplains, Chaplain (Major General) Sampson or Rabbi Maurice Lamm from the Jewish Welfare Board, all of us were involved in extending hospitality. On sacred occasions in all our calendars, invitations were extended to each other to attend and to learn. My colleagues were present at our Chanukah party and again sat at our seder on Passover. Truly I felt I was a full partner.

The full extent of fraternity was revealed when I traveled. The Christian chaplain was often the first one to greet me at the airstrip and to introduce me to others especially when I visited for the first time. I recall fondly being invited to share the "hooch" of the chaplains at Tuy Hoa, Song Mao, and Chu Lai, among others. Not yet knowing the Jewish members of local units, I depended on my Christian colleagues to point out the whereabouts of the men I sought. When it came time to reach out to Jewish personnel to come to gatherings on the High Holidays and Passover, it was often the Christian chaplain encouraging attendance. They were aware of special "times of obligation" in the Jewish calendar, and their mission included caring for non-Christians. I never once sensed a desire to proselytize among Jews.

I also had limited contact with Christians and Buddhists outside of the military. Along with other chaplains, I was invited to the home of a Christian missionary and his family. I described my visit to my wife:

*They have been here for most of the last thirteen years and impressed me as really dedicated people. They live in a large and beautiful home on a rise which looks out over the ocean. It is in Nha Trang on a large area owned by the Christian Missionary Alliance. They have a seminary, and Rev. Sutherland teaches there. He and his wife have four beautiful kids, and it was so nice to be with a family again. Other missionaries were there, too – mostly young, very idealistic and concerned. They gave us a warm welcome and especially tried to make me feel at home . . . Rev. Sutherland studied some Hebrew with rabbis years ago and wants to start again. He also suggests I come out to talk about Judaism with his classes. They served a sumptuous, barbecued chicken dinner and had tuna for me.*

I did teach at the seminary to Vietnamese students:

*My trip to the Protestant Seminary was a joy. It is in a beautiful setting on a rise overlooking Nha Trang. The audience was about 100 men and women, very friendly and attentive. Spence Sutherland, the missionary who invited me, stood at my side to translate, and it went remarkably smoothly. I showed them some books, my tefillin, and gave them some matza to try. I tried to cover a great deal and even ended up singing something from Hallel (psalms of praise recited on joyful occasions)! Once before a rabbi had sung for them, and they really enjoyed it. Incidentally, I didn't get to speak about Jewish attitudes toward Jesus. I talked with a student afterwards who had some questions and wondered about new Biblical materials that were available. He is a student of Hebrew and Greek and speaks English well. We hoped to meet again.*

I had one more extraordinary experience one day in January flying back from Pleiku. I wrote:

*I met a couple, civilians, traveling with a small baby. The name of the baby is... (hang on!) . . . DAVID COHEN!! No, he isn't. It's some story. The father is an evangelical Christian missionary working on Bible translation (into the local language). His great grandparents were German-Jewish. When they came to Alaska in about 1900 it seems they converted to become Episcopalian. That's on his (the baby's) mother's side . . . so he may be Jewish himself. In addition, his father was Irish and as a baby was orphaned and was brought up by a Jewish family named COHEN! Later he adopted the name for himself, and that's how the baby got his name. They are nice people with a darling baby but definitely not Jewish.*

While I knew that missionary work often took advantage of vulnerable people, I did feel good in their company.

The interfaith component of the chaplaincy would be a positive gift of my military experience. I brought that valuable model into the life of the civilian communities I would serve.

# 10 Connections to the Vietnamese

*Open air market in Nha Trang*

The damage that the war brought to Vietnam was evident. I knew about the ravages of Agent Orange in the countryside. I know that the consequences of exposure to Agent Orange continue to this day with new generations of babies born with major disabilities and deformities. I understand that the impact has been discovered in Laos as well where Agent Orange was also used for deforestation. I could not be unaware of civilian casualties which were inevitable. In my travels, I recall seeing civilians who were horribly crippled and maimed. While I could not be certain, I knew that some of the disfiguring I saw was the result of our war making. While the count of Americans killed was terribly high, it was far exceeded by Vietnamese

86

military forces and civilians who died. I recall one day traveling from Pleiku to Cam Ranh Bay and being asked to disembark from a flight to accommodate many coffins of South Vietnamese soldiers killed in battle and their families. I wrote to my wife:

*What a tragic sight that is to see the flag-draped coffins and the women and small children dressed in their white mourning garments. How they suffer here.*

As for the enemy, as in every war, they were totally dehumanized. On occasion, I was included in daily briefings conducted before senior staff and the commanding officers. I was disturbed at this glimpse of what seemed to really matter. After a briefing at Landing Zone English, I wrote:

*I went to a briefing where all the incidents today were reported – so many little things, booby traps, sniping. Life seems so insignificant here. Body counts mean a lot. No one seems to see that each one means a world destroyed.*

I craved more contact with ordinary Vietnamese. At airports, I often saw civilian families traveling together with their adorable children. I was impressed with the loving relationships between parents and children and the visible reverence for elders. Without a shared language, it was still possible to exchange smiles or gestures of enjoyment at the antics of children. I remember playing discreetly with a beautiful six-year-old girl with glances, winks, and smiles while she was waiting with her parents for their flight. I wrote about her:

*Aboard the airplane. My little friend is sitting beside me . . . She and I have become friends. I bought her some ice cream, and she gave me a stick of Juicy Fruit Gum and just offered me a hot dog! Wow, do I have charm with little girls!*

It was on another long flight that I had the opportunity to meet a captain in the Vietnamese Army who spoke excellent English. I wrote:

*He works in PSYOPS (psychological operations), came from North Vietnam, and seems passionately anti-Communist. He is a college man and seemed very well informed. He knew about Jews and told me that all the refugees fleeing from the North in 1954 were known as Jews because they were homeless. He told me about some of the hardships they face. His salary as a captain doesn't even pay for his own meals each month. His wife and child (both beautiful) live in Saigon and are cared for by parents on both sides. He sees her every six months or so. He amazed me with his tenacity to fight on until the last drop of blood. I questioned him about how he can face such a bleak future with indefinitely continuous war. He answered he is prepared. He seemed very friendly to Americans and appreciates our presence. He invited me over to his office whenever I can come...The contrast between our positions (both army captains) is unbelievably stark. It's the first time I've seen such feeling against Communism; but, again, I haven't had too much contact with Vietnamese.*

One day returning in the evening to my quarters, I came upon a group of Vietnamese children gathered around an obviously broken bicycle. I stopped to see if I could help. Regrettably one wheel was so misshapen that I concluded that it could not be repaired and probably should be replaced. I walked away feeling bad that I was not a skilled bicycle repairman.

While some units worked closely with the South Vietnamese Army, we had little contact of substance with those living around us. Our most frequent contact was with the many Vietnamese employed doing mostly menial work. In our office and in my room, Vietnamese women scrubbed, dusted, and polished. My uniforms were always promptly laundered and ironed. One day, I wrote to my wife:

*I went back to the hotel to pay my "hootch-maid." I gave her 1500 piastres – more than usual for a month, but I told her that 500 were for her new baby. She has been back working now for about three weeks and is really great. My clothes (underwear, towels, tzitzit, my undershirt with ritual*

88

*fringes) are washed daily, boots polished, room cleaned, even my canteen
filled sometimes. The exchange is about 118 piastres to the dollar – so really
it's not much anyway by our standards.*

I observed that most GIs treated these workers with respect. I know that
some sought opportunities to express gratitude with words and gifts.

I shared some of my frustration with my wife:

*I finished reading Vietnam: The Unheard Voices by Luce and Somner,
two young volunteers who spent years in Vietnam . . . We came out sorrowfully
mistaken in our approaches, but the book is sensitive about American motives
and the part we could have played constructively here.*

*I have so little contact with the people. I sure do hope we can organize
a little cultural series for the men in the compound in Nha Trang. It would
do us all good just to listen, one of the central themes in the book. I wish I
could contribute a little more to the people than the situation seems to allow.*

For the most part, however, we lived amidst the Vietnamese without
speaking their language or knowing anything about their faith and their
culture. The Army did publish some materials to acquaint us with our
neighbors, but scant attention was given to building awareness and sensibility
in an ongoing way.

I was asked to lead "Character Guidance" sessions, and one session
I recall was entitled "Social Concern." I described what transpired to my
wife:

*We talked quite a bit about what that would mean with regard to us
and Vietnamese. And the discussion went better than I expected. Many
feel themselves to be unavoidably ugly Americans. Some had insight I was
surprised at. One fellow mentioned that we degrade people when we go
into a house and shack up with a mother or sister. I don't know how many
secretly shuddered at that, but I thought it was a vocal expression aspect of
concern.*

All in all, what we did to reach out seemed thoroughly insufficient. I did try to introduce more knowledge of and contact with the Vietnamese around us into the Jewish program and beyond. However, we never succeeded in creating an ongoing program. It seemed that the war effort and meeting other basic needs left little energy to pursue a more humane approach to our neighbors.

What was heartening to me was to find individuals who did heroic work on their own. The toll of war left many orphans in the country, at times scratching out a meager existence in the streets totally on their own. One local unit in Nha Trang tried to look out for one small group of these children. I wrote to my wife:

*There is a new guy, a Catholic assistant, who is a really fine guy. Very motivated – caring – a real sense of service to others. He had in his barracks at a place where he had been two Vietnamese orphans, two boys about ten years old. When he left, he wrote home to his parents, asking if they would like to adopt them! He showed me their response – one of the most beautiful letters I have ever read. They have decided to take them. Such examples of giving – an act that commits them for a lifetime – makes me stop and feel inspired and wonder whether I would ever be as generous as they.*

One day, John Kanarek, this young assistant announced the adoption to our staff. We inquired how this had come about, and he explained: "I shared the plight of the kids with my parents. On the spot, they decided to take them into their family without knowing more about their background." They said to their son: "When you were conceived, it was the result of a spontaneous act of love between us. Now, our decision is simply one more spontaneous act of love." I was witness to a transcendent act of devotion!

I was simply overcome with admiration for these two parents ready to give themselves fully even later in life to salvage the lives of these children. Why was I not surprised later when the young assistant approaching the end of his tour came into our office to introduce a young Filipino woman working in Vietnam to whom he was engaged to be married?

Caring for the children who paid a steep price in this war seemed so urgent. Chaplain Paul Cassibry, a Protestant attached to a unit in Ban Me Thuot, organized a project for orphans connected to the 23rd Division of the South Vietnamese army. They were the children of soldiers killed in action. The goal was to collect candy and children's clothing. I asked Lorri if she could engage the youth group in the synagogue back home to join in this campaign. They were eager to join, and they did contribute substantially.

As Christmas approached, a joint choir of Protestant and Catholic men from our chapel in Nha Trang practiced a rich medley of Christmas music. On Christmas Eve, I recalled:

*A group of guys just got back from a caroling trip to several orphanages and hospitals, and are they enthused! They got such a warm response from the kids who climbed all over them. They felt so good about being with the people, something which the guys rarely get a chance to do.*

I remember meeting a young Black psyops officer in Song Mao who admitted he was against the war. He had learned Vietnamese, and he was intent on lending a helping hand to the community around him by improving a village for orphans and much more. Army engineers dug wells, built desks for school classrooms, and even built an addition for a leprosarium.

On the other side of the ledger, I learned sorrowfully that GIs were partially and directly responsible for a subset of orphans. I wrote to my wife:

*I understand that orphanages are a new thing in Vietnam. Before, kids were always somehow absorbed by the extended family. But now there is some breakdown there, and I hear that many of the kids are babies of Vietnamese girls and GIs, Black and white. They are ostracized and unwanted.*

Among those who made a difference even if it was outside of their responsibility was Henry Scheingold, the commander of an airbase near Pleiku. I wrote about him to my wife:

*I've come to like him very much. He is unlike many officers. He is unassuming, seems to deeply care for the men, and do you know how he spends most of his time? He is involved in many civic action projects which he does with real passion. Today he attended two dedications of schools for Montagnards. He supplied the materials, and they did the work. It is so good to see such a man, and he feels that what he does is part of his heritage as a Jew. Next time I come in September, he invited me over to take a tour of the area to see some of his pet projects.*

In the same area in Pleiku, I was given a tour by Dr. Albie Hornblass of a regional hospital where he and fellow physicians worked. I wrote about these doctors:

*They are giving of themselves to these people. These doctors have done so much – though they are often frustrated by the old ways of the people and at times a seeming lack of appreciation. The hospital is run down, dirty, and poor by our standards, but there is progress. You see everything in the wards. When a patient comes in, the whole family comes along. They prepare the food for the patients and stay with them constantly. I saw Montagnard tribesmen – women bare-breasted – who look like American Indians of the old West. They are primitive, but I understand they are very honest and straight . . . I would sure love to be able to really communicate with them. I'm trying to pick up a few words.*

In the chaos surrounding the end of the war and the flight of many from Vietnam, we learned that many orphaned children needed adoption. My wife and I looked at each other and decided to offer our home and family. We knew it would be difficult to integrate such a child into an observant Jewish home, but we were inspired by what I had seen firsthand. We inquired, and we discovered regrettably that we were not qualified. We felt a pull to step forward because of the severe price the war had exacted on the land and on the Vietnamese. We were heartened by the many Vietnamese refugees who found an open door to resettlement in the U.S. I relish meeting them to this day. They reminded me very much of Jewish immigration to this country and the trying steps needed to establish themselves in a new land.

# 11 Care from the Jewish Community

*Rabbi Lamm of JWB arrives*

Our program benefited immensely from caring agencies and people from across the United States. My office was never quite in order, nor was there extra space to navigate because of the largesse bestowed on us. The National Jewish Welfare Board (NJWB) in New York made certain that we had the resources that we needed. For those who kept kosher, we were able to provide regular deliveries mostly of canned Hebrew National products. On Rosh Hashanah and Passover, we received more than enough kosher TV dinners to serve everyone attending. While they were not freshly prepared, they were a source of delight to soldiers so far from home. We were literally sent everything from soup to nuts (to prepare charoset)! In addition, we had ample prayer books and copies of the Torah to distribute liberally. No special holiday was without its special symbols and ritual objects. As a chaplain, I also received a quarterly stipend from the JWB to supplement my military salary.

The JWB was not the only source of support. It is hard to count the Jewish veterans' organizations, the youth groups, women's groups from B'nai Brith, Jewish Welfare Board Auxiliaries, synagogue sisterhoods and more who filled my office with cards, gifts, salamis by the score, and home-made baked goods. One women's group in New Jersey sent us sufficient honey cakes for Rosh Hashanah to provide one complete honey cake for every attendee! A certain Mrs. Levy also from New Jersey was known all over Vietnam for sending salamis and cans of home-baked pastries to Jewish soldiers for seven and one-half years and running! My wife, my mother and my mother-in-law baked non-stop to provide snacks for every program and kiddush. In all, we had generous donors from Ohio, Tennessee, Washington State, California, Illinois, Mississippi, Massachusetts, New York, and New Jersey. Each delivery carried the message that we were not forgotten.

*Welcoming Rabbi Lamm with Dr. Joshua Sternberg*

The visit of Rabbi Maurice Lamm from the JWB was surely a highlight. During a whirlwind tour, he traveled to each of the three centers served by rabbis to offer his support and to meet personally with many of the men active in our programs. He met the commanding generals and the staff chaplains in each headquarters as well. In my area, he visited our groups in Qui Nhon, Cam Ranh Bay, and Nha Trang. We served him meals largely prepared from the stock of supplies we received from the JWB, Hebrew National canned meats supplemented by our own creativity. Here is the menu we served him and 25-30 men active in our program:

*Grapefruit Sections with a Cherry*
*Sweet & Sour Stuffed Cabbage*
*Meat Ball Hoagies*
*Tossed Salad*
*Baked Potatoes*
*Iced Tea*
*Peaches*

Surely his presence lifted the morale of us all.

When it came time for Rabbi Lamm to depart, we handed him a corned beef sandwich on rye for the road! Never did he imagine such a treat in Nha Trang! How did we manage such a treat? The source was my wife who found numerous ingenious ways to supplement our diet!

# 12 Coping

For much of my life before Vietnam, my emotional state was mostly steady and upbeat without frequent steep peaks and valleys. I was not prepared for what service in the war zone would bring.

Facing each day in Vietnam summoned levels of coping deep within myself I was uncertain I possessed. I had never been challenged as I would be during that year. I knew that I needed to either take hold and grow in maturity, or I would sink into despair. Since my mission was to lift the spirits of the men I served, my success depended on my ability to control my own wild mood swings.

Shared with so many, my primary source of misery was my loneliness, being so far from my wife, family, and friends. My letters home expressed my changes in spirit. Here I was caught in a morally fraught universe so far from home and unsure that I could make a difference while thoughts of those I missed horribly were always close at hand. I felt very fragile. I tried to conceal my personal anguish when I was with others. At least my purpose in Vietnam was meaningful to me. For others, their missions which ran the spectrum from boring to meaningless to morally questionable only added to their pain.

I did lean on my personal religious commitments: daily prayer, learning Torah, and sacred times for comfort and uplift. They are powerful and soothing. Yet I found that ironically Shabbat and holidays so far from vital communities did, at times, add to my burden. The best of times could become the worst of times.

My highest moments were either at mail-call or when I was immersed in my work. The Army surely recognized how vital the mail system would be for morale. Routinely we had mail in our compound twice each day, at 11 AM and again at 5 PM. Of course, when mail with my name on it was distributed, especially in my wife's handwriting, I was elated. When inevitably there were days with nothing for me or when I was traveling and away at mail call, I was saddened. Bad weather or even the tragic crash of a plane carrying mail in Okinawa interrupted the normal flow. We were tethered to those fragile connections to those back home.

I felt most vital when I was with the people I was serving, especially on a one-on-one basis. When I returned to my quarters after meeting with individuals, or after a kiddush or class, my spirits soared. I wrote to my wife:

*The best was just to sit and talk with these men. I thrive on that. You know, I value more than ever simple human contact. When I am with a guy and simply talk, honestly and without reserve, I am the happiest I can be here.*

If I could have been engaged continually with others, I would have thrived. There were many evenings when discussions went on hour after hour. I think we did not want them to end lest we had to face the painful realities around us once more.

A letter, an audio tape, or an occasional phone call and being with others one-on-one or in a group were the sources of joy for me. Time alone to reflect was most often a descent into sadness.

I also was worn down by the realities of travel in a war zone. Uncounted days found me facing long holdovers at air terminals when flights were delayed for many hours or cancelled altogether. More than once programs had to be cancelled or rescheduled because of the vagaries of air travel. In one of many similar descriptions of flight uncertainties, I wrote:

*Today was another of what seemed to be increasingly frustrating days. I spent half the day at the airport awaiting my return flight. The monsoons bring constant rain and low cloud ceilings, and so many flights are cancelled or delayed for long periods. I wish I could avoid the airports a little more . . . but . . .*

Even telephone contact could create a wide range of emotion. The fact that we could speak at all directly from Vietnam to loved ones was a great blessing. The ham radio network (known as MARS, the Military Amateur Radio System) was a marvel of cooperation between the military and willing volunteers across the United States. The calls were limited to 3 minutes, and they were not private. Yet the sound of my wife's voice, even as distorted or cut off as it might be, provided rare moments of being in touch in real time. These were high moments.

I frequently arose early in the morning to place a call as I awaited contact from the MARS station. When my wife was visiting my parents, I was determined to place a call which failed. I wrote to her:

*I'm so sorry. I came into the office at 6:15 this morning to be first on the list to call and waited all morning only to discover that no calls went out because of problems with the radio equipment . . . I feel so badly because I know you and the folks must have stayed home just waiting. I could picture you, after all the promises I made to call.*

So very often the system was down, and the call could not be placed. The day would begin with hopes that were ultimately unfulfilled. Still, I was grateful for the possibility of contact.

Occasionally a special opportunity presented itself. I described it to my wife:

*I was invited to visit Fred Miller, a great guy who is in charge of the switchboard at Cam Rahn Bay. We were just visiting when he asked if I would like to call you. I knew you would be in a deep sleep, but this was my one chance to talk normally and for more than three minutes so I was sure you would be glad, too, once you were awake. I wish I could have forewarned you just a little.*

The call did shock my wife, but it was a high moment that came out of nowhere!

Even R & R and leave could bring precipitous swings in spirit. Joyful reunions with my wife were inevitably followed by anguished separations. Of course, even knowing that the pain would follow would not deter us from every moment together we could muster. We simply learned to fortify ourselves for the letdown that would follow every meeting.

I know that I was not alone in feeling I was engaged in two wars, one outwardly in the war zone and the other inwardly facing personal anguish. Once sitting in a small library in Nha Trang, I found a Shakespearian sonnet (#29) that captured my feelings. I shared these words with my wife:

*When, in disgrace with fortune and men's eyes.*
*I all alone beweep my outcast state.*
*And trouble deaf heaven with my bootless cries.*
*And look upon myself and curse my fate,*
*Wishing me like to one more rich in hope, . . .*
*Yet in these thoughts myself almost despising,*
*Haply I think on thee, and then my state,*
*Like to the lark at break of day arising*
*From sullen earth, sings hymns at heaven's gate;*
*For thy sweet love rememb'red such wealth brings*
*That then I scorn to change my state with kings.*

CHAPTER 13 Going Home

*Flying Tigers – Flying Home*

When the time approached for me to return home, I composed a final message in our monthly bulletin.

*This letter will be my last to you before my DEROS in just a few weeks. I feel the mixed emotions we all experience when about to depart, a combination of unbounded joy and complete happiness. I am terribly excited.*

*As I look back over the year, there were many moments I will remember: celebrations of holidays we shared, conversation over some precious ethnic morsels, a good laugh which helped us all to forget, meeting at an airport, a bit of truth about ourselves which we shared with one another, an expression of gratitude for a can of chicken soup, an animated discussion while studying together. There are certain parts of this year which I know we will not mind forgetting but not the people. You, my congregation, are now my friends; . . . and I feel sure that we have a bond which will make us feel close whenever our paths cross in the years to come. I sincerely hope that we will meet again in another far different setting. I will especially remember the dedication of my assistants, and your lay leaders, the hospitality each of you showed me on my rounds, and your positive responses as Jews. These qualities of yours have made this year a little easier, a little less lonely for me, I only hope that our program has helped you in some small measure, too.*

*Remember that wherever I have my congregation back home, you will find an open door and a good Shabbat meal. My Lorri is already dreaming up recipes. I even guarantee a special deal on membership in my shul. My best wishes to you always.*

As I prepared to leave, I imagined myself returning to the causes in which I longed to be involved. I wrote:

*I begin to see how these two years have taken me away from so many things and issues that I want to be active in. Maybe if anything, this year will help give me more of a grounding in experience so that my feelings are a little more well-grounded. How I hate this war – what it's doing to this country and to us.*

Arriving in Cam Ranh Bay to meet my flight home, I was more than ready to hand over my uniforms and my jungle boots, the best made footwear I have ever worn. I waited patiently in the inevitable line for customs and the search for drugs. Boarding a bus, we all sat on the edge of our seats until we came upon the huge Flying Tigers jet which would take us home. The takeoff was one of the most exhilarating moments in my life.

# 14 The Aftermath

*Visiting with Lloyd Kantor after
coming home, circa 1975*

On the long flight home from Cam Ranh Bay to McChord Air Force Base near Tacoma, I struggled to make sense of the year. Rabbi Eugene Borowitz, editor of "Shma" had asked for my reflections on the chaplaincy in Vietnam, my expectations and my experiences. Before sitting down to write, I had shared my thoughts with my wife:

*I have felt a reluctance to write up to now – somehow being a little too bewildered to sort out my feelings and especially the moral issues. But, while I feel so much ambivalence toward the chaplaincy now, still I want to help and to talk to others, and I do feel its importance. I have to admit that much of my bewilderment is as much the personal hurts of being away and isolated as it is the moral and spiritual limitations and concessions in being in the army.*

Finally, I wrote for Shma:

*Sitting in the full but almost silent flight which was to bring me home from Vietnam, I was troubled by thoughts of how to respond to questions that*

102

were certain to come. *"How do you feel now about the war?" "How has the experience changed your point of view?" "What is the truth about Vietnam?"* I found it was more difficult for me to talk about the war than it had been two years earlier before entering the chaplaincy. Even in anticipation, I was stammering. The words and thoughts and judgments simply had to be forced.

Now I realize that my grasping for words about war is perhaps one of the consequences of serving as a chaplain. The two years were a time of silence, of distance from the protest movement, of being unable to voice publicly my revulsion for Vietnam. My writing and teaching avoided moral issues which otherwise would have been central. Now it was so difficult to find the words, to pick up a train of thought long neglected. It was as if a certain area of my ability to judge had atrophied and now had to be nurtured anew. Yet if I were to face the same choice which I had made two years ago, I would not hesitate to go the same route.

If anything, this period in uniform has made the issue of the chaplaincy more complex for me than it had been before. I would insist now that one really does give up some of his ethical autonomy and that one learns about the meaning of compromise firsthand. When I entered the army, I came into a context with a pre-programmed moral valence. The direction of the military became mine. Regardless of how I would see my role as a rabbi, I always knew that I was contributing to the Army's goals. If I were to do my job at all, I would be helping my men to be better soldiers and to be a little more at peace within themselves.

While I never picked up a weapon or had to rally men into battle, I was furthering the aims of a military enterprise to which I could not subscribe at all. Even the presence of a rabbi has that effect. My personal intent to serve the needs of Jews in a more limited sense could only be separated cerebrally from the larger picture.

*Yet today it is just that principle of moral autonomy whose value I question. For a rabbi, it almost seems itself immoral. The role of rabbi implies for me an interconnectedness with fellow Jews, the sharing of the crises which face the Jews of this generation. That role necessarily contains a certain limitation on our personal freedom if insistence on our being untainted severs contact with our brethren. Today rabbinical students and young rabbis are really the only group who can live their lives without ever facing the issue of military service. The dilemma which plagues the formative years of most young men, the often-excruciating delays and redirection of lifetime plans caused by the imminence of the draft is unknown to the man who decides to enter the rabbinate. Unless he steps forward by volunteering or by actively joining in draft and war protest, he passes unscathed. This inequity which places Vietnam and military service at such a comfortable, theoretical distance from the rabbinate, makes me uncomfortable. There is a need to respond to this imbalance although I know that my response is by no means the only one. It seems to me indisputable that some response is even an obligation.*

*That, as a rabbi, I must be with Jews wherever they are and in whatever activity they are engaged seems to me untenable. But those who are today in the service have a special claim upon us. Most are not moral giants; neither are they criminals. They reject radical action and enter the service because the law requires them to serve. Yet they bring with them all their feelings of ambivalence and doubt about Vietnam and the military which most young men harbor. They do not choose to be where they are, and therefore all the normal problems of adjustment of a human being in a war zone are complicated and intensified.*

*Such men deserve special attention. I found that I had to reorient some of my most precious goals as a rabbi. I had to get used to a constantly transient congregation, widely scattered, and I found I could not develop an ongoing program of learning and observance over any substantial period. The faces were ever-changing; the contacts were fleeting. Not uncommon was a whole day's journey to see two or three men or Shabbat spent with half a minyan. Yet being with those few men seemed to me to be important. Even if we shared no religious concerns, we did have many common bonds, and dialogue was almost always possible. At least we could share our misery. Often there was no one else to whom a Jewish man could talk, and certainly there was no other religious influence. Not once during the year did one of the men ask me why it was I had come. They seem to know.*

*For some, the pressures of each day sometimes exploded into a crisis. I particularly remember those times, being with a man who just a few hours before had lost all his limbs when a booby trap was triggered, spending time with a group of guys in shock at the death of a buddy just days before he was to go home, sitting with a man who had killed five or six human beings and now could no longer stomach the war or maybe himself, trying to comfort a man who just heard that his wife had become pregnant back home, 9,000 miles away. I cannot imagine how terrifying it could be to have to face these tragedies all by oneself.*

*God willing, Vietnam and the compulsory draft will soon be past. Until that day however, the chaplaincy must receive a high priority in our commitments. It is not even desirable that every man volunteer, but I feel it is the responsibility of all to see that our chaplaincy quotas are met. However, we feel about the war, regardless of how we might abhor the military's direction, the men in uniform cannot be abandoned.*

*The Psalmist writes: Even God suffers with His people.*

*Can we, as rabbis, afford to do any less?*

I was also invited to weigh in on the debate of whether divinity students of every faith should be exempt from the draft. I was expected to support the continuing exclusion, but I had reservations. I wrote:

*I felt I couldn't support it strongly, so I thought I better not write at all. I've long felt uneasy about the total exemption. I feel a deferment is important – but to make us the only ones who are forever exempt just strikes me as not good. If a man after finishing his ordination feels so strongly he cannot serve in the military, he does have recourse to the C.O. position. But as long as we have the draft and all the other guys must suffer with it, I feel uncomfortable with the exemption. It was one of the main reasons I came into the Army. I'm afraid that many of the guys never face the agony of dealing with the military because the law does not force one to confront the reality.*

*With Lloyd Kantor*

# CHAPTER 15 Final Thoughts

*Lloyd and Loretta Kantor with the rabbi and his wife, Lorri*

When I look back at my younger self fifty years ago trying to cope as a rabbi with all the challenges of living in a war zone, I am astonished with how little I have changed. I do not have second thoughts about the decision I made then. My attitude toward war and my commitment to my fellow Jews in distress have not changed. Twenty-eight years old and having just been ordained, I could have benefitted from more experience with life itself. I could have used more wisdom and more learning to bring to bear on the awful stresses faced by the special people in uniform I met in Vietnam.

Surely my witnessing the carnage in Vietnam on the bodies and souls of combatant and civilian alike and on the land itself strengthens my abhorrence of war. I try to imagine what life might have been like for those who were injured outwardly or inwardly, what possibilities were forcefully taken from them due to the war. What journeys, joys, adventures, contributions, and aspirations were thwarted? With the frightful toll of lives cut off, uncounted dreams were ended. Entire worlds in the eyes of Jewish tradition were destroyed. This price seems way too steep in a war that was immoral. I am not a pacifist when there is a need to defend oneself from harm. Yet this was a war that should have been avoided.

Of course, there will be passionate disputes among the peoples of the world. Every form of communication and diplomacy should be the tools for resolution rather than a resort to arms.

When I left Vietnam and the Army, I did not leave behind some of the special relationships that were formed in the vortex of war and trauma. Lloyd and Loretta Kantor live a vibrant life today. What was taken from Lloyd fifty years ago was substantial, but his wounds did not erase the hopeful, optimistic, energetic, vital spirit that is most essentially who he is. I know of few people who have such a rich sense of humor! Loretta is fully his match and his tireless helpmate. To be with this couple is to be with a resilient, relentless life force which continues to inspire me and my wife. I witnessed scenes that I wished I had never seen, that had never happened; but I have also been able to see a heroic aftermath which truly inspires. Friendship with the Kantors is a great gift.

We are still in recovery from the tragic period of the war in Vietnam. I know that some wounds linger for a lifetime, outer and less visible injuries, too. Yet given the conditions of that war, I was privileged to know men and women who found ingenious ways to cope. They always counted the days until their names were called to board a flight for home, but many made the days bearable by supporting one another, by doing acts of kindness for the Vietnamese people around them, by using their skills to heal and to save lives such as Lloyd's, and by allowing their Jewish heritage to bring comfort with something as small as an ethnic morsel that did more than nourish the body or as large as entering a sacred time when time around them was empty and painful. Jewish life seemed to provide a lifeline, a reminder of normality. We were strengthened by the basic values and practices of our faith while we were so far from home.

# Acknowledgements

Attempting to recapture memories after fifty years, I needed help. I have been richly blessed with the support of family and friends who encouraged me and contributed generously to make this memoir possible.

I am grateful to my readers who read drafts of my manuscript with care and whose suggestions greatly refined my work. My esteemed team includes Joel Brauner, Rabbi Ari Cartun, Rabbi Amy Eilberg, Dr. Bruce Feldstein, Ed Finkelstein, Elisheva Goldstein, Mark Gumbiner, Kim Howard, Rev. Doug Huneke, Ted and Frona Kahn, Lloyd and Loretta Kantor, Rabbi Maurice Kaprow, Professor Hillel Levine, my sons Akiva and Shalom Lewis, my wife Lorri, my twin brother Sherwin Lewis, my sister and brother-in-law Linda and Bruce Mayor, and Rabbi Fred Wenger.

Lloyd, Ed, Joel, and Fred were there with me in Vietnam, and they shared deeply the stresses and agonies of that period. The book is dedicated to Lloyd and his wife Loretta who are prominent in my narrative and whose resilience in the face of grievous wounds inspires me every day.

My friend Miriam Schulman has a keen editorial eye, and she graciously and carefully read my draft. Her gentle and thoughtful suggestions are in evidence on almost every page. I am grateful for her generosity.

I have come to depend on Rashida Basrai for formatting my work with such skill and sensitivity. There is magic when she sets her hand to a manuscript. She is a cherished friend.

I am grateful to Hakodesh Press for actively seeking manuscripts and embracing my sixth book that they have brought to publication. I appreciate my editor, Catalina Popoveniuc, for always being positive, prompt, and eager to offer assistance.

I never was a devoted journal writer, so the record of my year in Vietnam had to come from another source. I was a devoted letter writer to my dear wife. Our first year of marriage was spent separated from each other due to my deployment. She was my lifeline, and I opened my heart to her to share what I experienced. Those letters, profusely drawn upon in these pages, became my main source of memory. I am so grateful that she has been my life partner from then until this day, 51 years later.

It remains a source of wonder to be able to reflect on events one half century ago. I am eternally grateful to the Creator Who has watched over me and enabled me to reach this day.

Printed by
**Schaltungsdienst Lange o.H.G., Berlin**